TYPOLOGY AND THE GOSPEL

George Wesley Buchanan

ľłK

UNIVERSITY
PRESS OF
AMERICA

Lanham • New York • London

Copyright © 1987 by

University Press of America,® Inc.

4720 Boston Way
Lanham, MD 20706

3 Henrietta Street
London WC2E 8LU England

British Cataloging in Publication Information Available

Library of Congress Cataloging-in-Publication Data

Buchanan, George Wesley.
  Typology and the Gospel.

  Bibliography: p.
  Includes index.
  1. Bible. N.T. Gospels—Relation to the Old
Testament, Hexateuch. 2. Bible. O.T. Hexateuch—
Relation to the Gospels. 3. Typology (Theology)
I. Title.
BS2555.2.B78   1987   226'.064   87-8276
ISBN 0-8191-6377-5 (alk. paper)
ISBN 0-8191-6378-3 (pbk. : alk. paper)

All University Press of America books are produced on acid-free
paper which exceeds the minimum standards set by the National
Historical Publication and Records Commission.

To My Wonderful Aunt

RUBY BUCHANAN SHIELDS

ACKNOWLEDGEMENTS

The relationship of typologies to gospels was first brought to my attention by Austin Farrer and C. F. Evans, both of whose works are documented in this study. The comparison of Jesus in the Fourth Gospel with Elijah and Elisha in First and Second Kings has been taken almost verbatim from GWB, "The Samaritan Origin of the Gospel of John," Religions in Antiquity, ed. J. Neusner (Leiden: E. J. Brill, 1968):149-75. In chapter one, "Forerunners of the Gospel," is a brief section, "Time and Cycles." This is a much abbreviated and adapted version of a topic which was treated in a whole chapter, "Cycles of Time and their Signs," in GWB, Jesus: the King and his Kingdom (Macon: Mercer U. Press, c1984). A few pages from the article, "The Samaritan Origin of the Gospel of John," were also quoted in Jesus: The King and his Kingdom, pp. 304-308. These works have both been used here with permission and appreciation. I also appreciate the contribution made to this volume by my wife, Harlene. She has proof read this manuscript several times and assisted in the preparation of the index. Unless otherwise indicated, all translations in this volume are mine.

CONTENTS

FORERUNNERS OF THE GOSPEL

PREFACE

Years of study have increasingly impressed upon me the strong influence of typology in Jewish and Christian thought. So many later characters, deeds, and prophecies seem to have been based on earlier characters, deeds, and convictions that the phenomenon cannot have been accidental. There was some basic belief related to all of this that prompted the ancient Near Easterners to think, write, and believe in typological concepts. This brief and sketchy report shows some facts, analyses, and hypotheses that are related to typology. Among them are the Jewish concepts of time and the repetition of deliverances, such as those from Egypt, Babylonia, and the Greeks. These deliverances are reflected in the literary structure of the documents called Christian gospels. Conclusions reached in this kind of literary and historical analysis are necessarily tentative and suggestive rather than absolute. Nevertheless they are thought-provoking and may inspire readers to gain more insights than those suggested here.

I have postponed publication of these suggestions, hoping to gain bases for more solid solutions and conclusions, but further insights have not been forthcoming, so I have decided to publish these in this form, with the hope that others may clarify the problem better and offer more satisfying conclusions than I have done. One of the reasons, however, that conclusions are not easily reached that will satisfy Western scientific analysts is that the material was never prepared for such readers. Both readers and writers were apologists, dogmatists, sytematic theologians. They were religiously convinced in advance of the conclusions that were shown. It does not require much evidence to persuade those already convinced. They can ignore all difficulties and cling fast to whatever straws seem to appear.

This project is dedicated to my Aunt Ruby whose kindnesses to me have been too many, too great, and over too long a period to be listed. All of my research reflects the influence of my wife, Harlene, whose encouragement and affection makes research worthwhile. To both of these I am very grateful.

CHAPTER ONE

FORERUNNERS OF THE GOSPEL

INTRODUCTION

The New Temple. When Eusebius gave the keynote address for the dedication of the new church at Tyre, he spoke in glowing terms as if this were Solomon's temple and Bishop Pausanius were the new Bezalel, Solomon, the king, and the new Zerubbabel.[1] This church was a divine tabernacle.[2] Tyre, in turn, was a new and better Jerusalem.[3] This practice of identifying later historical events and people with earlier ones was an old practice that is evident in literature such as the Pentateuch, as scholars have shown.

Egyptian Release. Daube,[4] for example, said that the Exodus pattern was by far the most important pattern of deliverance in the Bible, but instead of showing all of the ways in which this pattern had been imitated in later literature, Daube set out to show that the Exodus narrative itself was patterned after still earlier literature. Noting the many parallels between the Exodus story, on the one hand, and the rules governing release of debtor slaves on Sabbath and Jubilee years,[5] on the other, he argued convincingly that the author of the Exodus narrative wrote his story as if the release of the Hebrews from Egypt were the fulfillment of these commandments.

The author described the Hebrews as slaves away from home; he identified the Pharaoh as the slave owner who sent them away; and he pictured the Hebrews as those who had not been sent away empty handed. Pharaoh, of course, did not send them away with all these material assets knowingly or willingly. The Egyptians thought they were loaning these gifts to the Hebrews. It was God who forced the Egyptians to fulfill these laws of Sabbath release. Daube did not deduce from this that the Exodus author had composed this narrative after he had read Leviticus and Deuteronomy. He presumed that the Exodus story had been written earlier than these documents, but Daube believed there were written and unwritten laws upon which Deuteronomy had depended which had been accessible to the Exodus author as well. The author of the Exodus story, then, created the narrative to make it correspond to the requirements of a debtor slave's release on the Sabbath or Jubilee year. He referred to the Hebrews as "slaves"; he pictured Pharaoh as an

1

oppressive master who finally "sent" the Hebrews away, just as creditors were obligated to send away their debtor slaves; and he included details to fulfill the requirement that slaves not be sent away empty handed.

Slavery Laws. Carmichael[6] held that the dependency was just the reverse. The author of the Deuteronomic laws deduced from the Exodus narrative that this was the pattern of God's action. Since God had acted to release Hebrews from Egypt, sending these slaves out with adequate supplies, God expected Hebrews to deal with their slaves in the same way. Therefore, the author made laws which he believed were God's laws on the basis of God's action in relationship to slavery in Egypt. This means the Deuteronomist believed that the exodus from Egypt was a type of slavery release which Israelites should pattern.

Continuing this logic, Carmichael[7] has made a strong case for believing that the Deuteronomist deliberately composed his credo[8] with the intention of reminding those who recited it of three important events in earlier history: 1) Jacob/Israel sending messengers ahead to see if it were possible for him to enter the promised land,[9] 2) Israelites sending messengers into the promised land to see if it were possible to conquer the land,[10] 3) children of Israel sending messengers to the children of Esau to see if permission could be granted for them to pass through Edom on the way to the promised land.[11]

The Israelites were escaping bondage from Egypt just as Israel had been doing when he left Aram; Israelites had to confront Esauites before returning to the land, just as Jacob had to confront Esau; both Israel and the Israelites finally reached the promised land, but when they sent messengers to spy out the land at Kadesh, they found obstacles and were delayed, just as Israelites at Kadesh thirty-eight years later were detained when they sent out messengers to spy out the situation in Edom. The Deuteronomist, according to Carmichael, intentionally composed this credo so that when the celebrant offered his first fruits he thought of the first fruits which the messengers brought back to Kadesh and at the same time thought of both confrontations with Esau--one on the way from Aram and one on the way from Egypt. If the author of Deuteronomy actually composed his credo in this way, he was using earlier events as types after which to create antitypes, and in so doing impressed upon the minds of those who recited the creed this typological kind of

2

thinking. Whether or not the Deuteronomic credo was instrumental in promoting typology, typological thinking existed, continued, and is obvious, here and there, throughout the Bible.

Typology. "Typology" is a belief that objects, events, persons, and institutions exist and occur in relationship to other corresponding objects, events, persons, and institutions. Typology is the term used to describe these relationships. For earthly things, when considered antitypes, there were prior and corresponding heavenly prototypes or archetypes that were patterns by which the earthly things were created. When the typology dealt with earthly things, the pattern was usually referred to as the "type," rather than the "prototype," and its corresponding antitype was also earthly and historical. When NT authors used the typological method of exegesis, the "type" was in the Hebrew Scripture, and the "antitype" was in the NT interpretation.

The word "type" comes from the Greek typtein, "to strike." It has the basic meaning of a blow or a mark left by a blow or strike. It is like the impression left by a seal on wax. The impression, then, is the mold from which other seals or forms can be made. The instrument that made the impression, the striker or typer, was sometimes called the type, but the matrix that received the impression, was also called the type. The initial striker might be called the archetype, pattern, or model which could be imitated.[12] This succession of impressions could continue. For example, a heavenly prototype might make an earthly type or antitype, which, in turn could have corresponding types or antitypes.

Lampe criticized typology as an exegetical method. He held that it had some of the same problems as allegory and was sometimes little more than a rhetorical trick. For example, he noted that it was only by a far-fetched process of reasoning that Melchizedek could be held to be superior to the Levitical priesthood, but the primary typology claimed by the author of Hebrews between the high priest's actions on the Day of Atonement and those he ascribed to Jesus were genuine type and antitype.[13]

This study will not provide an exhaustive appraisal of all examples of typology in the Bible. It will point out some of them as illustrations, examine their function in literature, and study the cultural thought-forms required to use typology in the way ancient Jews and Christians did. If this were a doctrinal study it might be proper to consider whether or not typology used by biblical authors was far-fetched and/or a legitimate discipline for theologians to practice today, but this is basically a factual analysis. The question here is, "Did the biblical authors employ typology at all?" The answer to this question is clearly, "Yes." Some of the common biblical types are Elijah, Phinehas, Joseph, Jesus, the captivity, and release. These will be considered here.

TYPES AND ANTITYPES

Elijah Type. Elijah was a famous prophet in North Israel who performed many miracles, stood up in resistance to an idolatrous government, and cleansed the land from pagan priests.[14] At a later time, when the priests of Israel were judged to be corrupt, Malachi reasoned that a new Elijah was needed in his day to cleanse the priesthood again. Malachi, therefore, promised that the Lord would cleanse the land of these wicked priests who had broken the contract Levi had once made with the Lord. The Levite, said Malachi, was the messenger for the Lord of armies,[15] and in the day of judgment that was coming, the sons of Levi would be purified.[16] When the Lord returned to his temple, there would first be a messenger, an antitype of the old Levi with whom the Lord had made a contract. This new messenger would be an antitype also of Elijah.[17] From the time of Malachi on, Elijah was thought of as the Lord's messenger who would come before the Lord returned to his temple. There were several ramifications of this. The Lord would not return to the temple until the land was restored to the chosen people. At that time there would not only be a new temple, but also a high priest and a king, the Lord's anointed ones.

When Jesus referred to John as "Elijah," he meant that John the Baptist was the antitype of the type, Elijah. He functioned in the way Elijah was supposed to function. When Herod called Jesus, "John raised from the dead," he meant that Jesus was just another John the baptist or an antitype of the type, John.

Woollcombe distinguished among allegory, fulfillment of scripture, and typology. Allegory, he said, concentrates on details and is not historically controlled. He acknowledged that typology and fulfill-

4

ment of scripture sometimes overlap, but an event, such as the triumphal entry,[18] was not really typology but the fulfillment of Zech 9:9. Typology relates one historical event to another, not in details, but in basics. A question such as the one that John might be Elijah[19] was typological and not the fulfillment of scripture. John could not have fulfilled the prophecy that Elijah must first come, because he was not really Elijah. He was an antitype of Elijah. Woollcombe thought the term "recapitulate" was the best term to describe some of the prophecy fulfillments in the New Testament. For example, Jesus was held to be the recapitulation of the son of David and the son of Abraham. The temple in Ezekiel's vision was a recapitulation of Solomon's temple. The deliverance from Babylon was a recapitulation of the deliverance from Egypt.[20] We will not make that distinction here. These will be termed, "types," and the next type to be considered is Joseph.

The Joseph Type. For many years scholars have observed that the hero of Dan 2 has been clearly patterned after the Joseph stories in Gen 41. The following chart makes this obvious:

Daniel	Joseph
Nebuchadnezzar had a dream[21]	Pharaoh had a dream[22]
His spirit was troubled (tipaʿem ruḥo)[23]	His spirit was troubled (tipaʿem ruḥo)[24]
He called for the best wisemen in Babylon[25]	He called for the best wisemen in Egypt[26]
They could not interpret the dream[27]	They could not interpret the dream[28]
An official brought Daniel to the king[29]	An official brought Joseph to the Pharaoh[30]
Daniel interpreted the dream[31]	Joseph interpreted the dream[32]
Nebuchadnezzar praised Daniel's God[33]	Pharaoh acknowledged that Joseph was favored by God[34]
Daniel made ruler over all Babylon (ʿal kol medynat babel).[35]	Joseph made ruler over all Egypt (ʿal kol ʾereṣ Miṣraim).[36]

The Book of Daniel was composed as if Daniel had been a Jewish hero during the Babylonian diaspora, so it was easy for the author to look for a type to follow from an earlier diaspora in Egypt. Since Joseph was one of the heroes who saved Israel during its Egyptian diaspora so that the Israelites could escape and return at a later time, Daniel was intentionally caricatured to be a new Joseph—wise, courageous, pious, prudent, and law abiding. Like Joseph, Daniel faced many dangers, but God always delivered him from them and rewarded him handsomely. This historical novel encouraged Jews to believe that Jews in the Babylonian diaspora would be rescued again and would later return to the promised land. Woollcombe overlooked examples such as these when he held that historical typology came into existence with Christianity.[37]

Phinehas Type. At a time when Hebrews were suffering because they had mingled with the neighboring Gentiles, the priest, Phinehas, took the law in his own hands and killed two of the offenders.[38] The author of First Maccabees believed Mattathias, the patron of the Hasmoneans, was a new Phinehas, and he pictured him as killing the mingling Jew, together with the pagan foreigner. In the name of his forefather, Phinehas, he raised his sword and began to recruit zealous patriots in an effort to throw off the yoke of the foreign rule.[39]

These details may not all have been exactly as the author of First Maccabees gave them. There was the factual basis that Mattathias rebelled against the neighboring collaborators and ruling foreigners and led the Maccabean revolt. Since this was something like that done by Phinehas, the author of I Maccabees created a scene very much like the one in which Phinehas was the hero, even to the extent of having Mattathias kill two people as Phinehas had done—one a mingling Jew and the other a foreigner. Because this author understood the type-antitype concept, he told the story so that Mattathias fit the antitype very well.

Many centuries later, some midrashic rabbi believed that he lived in a destructive age, like the one faced by Phinehas and Mattathias. He derived comfort from Numbers 25, believing as he did that God would act in his day as he had in the past. There would be a new teacher of righteousness, an antitype of the priest Phinehas. He would act as Phinehas and Mattathias had done to purge the land from this foreign corruption. He interpreted Num 25 as follows:

When he [Phinehas] went out, he saw the angel striking the people with a plague. Thus it is written, but one sinner destroys [much good] (Eccles 9,18); this refers to Zimri, because of whom twenty-four thousand Israelites perished. When Phinehas executed judgment the plague was stopped, as it says, And Phinehas executed judgment (WYPLL PYNḤS) [so the plague was stopped] (Ps 106,30). WYPLL refers to judgment, for it is written, and he shall pay as the judges determine (NTN BPLYLYM) (Exod 21,22). So, may there come a teacher of righteousness in our lifetime and may he bring about judgment and justice in truth in the building up of Jerusalem, as it is written, The Lord builds up Jerusalem, etc. (Ps 147,2).[40]

The Hasmoneans functioned both as priests and government rulers, so the new teacher of righteousness could be both the military leader and also the high priest. When the new Phinehas came he would act just the way Mattathias and Phinehas had acted in the past. In this way Phinehas became a type of patriotic zealous rebel in whom Jewish zealots put their hopes. Elijah was the one anticipated in an expectation of two messiahs--one of Aaron and one of David--whereas Phinehas was the priest expected to function like the Levitical Hasmoneans. He was the type that motivated zealots to fight.

Jesus Type. Although Jesus was considered an antitype of Moses, Joshua, David, and Elisha, he himself was considered to be the type after which the apostles were patterned. It was not difficult for later authors to reason this way. An apostle is a legal agent who is legally identical to the principal for whom he or she is employed. This recognition was acknowledged by the author of Matthew who pictured Jesus as one who called people to repent because the Kingdom of Heaven was near (chapter 4). He was presented as the great teacher in chapters 5-7; the next chapters (8-9) showed Jesus healing and casting out demons. Chapter 10 is devoted to Jesus commissioning the twelve to do exactly that which he had been doing--teaching, healing, casting out demons, and announcing the nearness of the Kingdom of Heaven.

This typological conviction was basic to the author of Acts. For example, the man who had been blind from birth was healed at once by Jesus. This caused a great furor among the religious people who

7

tried to get the man to deny that he had been healed, but he refused.[41] Likewise Peter healed a lame man at the temple gate. Afterward the apostles were cross-examined by the high priest and other officials who tried to suppress Peter and quiet the excitement that had aroused the people.[42] To prove Paul's apostleship, the author also provided for him to heal a lame man.[43]

Jesus raised a girl who had died by saying, "Talitha, arise," "Little girl, arise!"[44] and Peter did the same thing, saying, "Tabitha, arise!"[45] A woman touched the hem of Jesus' garment and was healed from her hemorrhage.[46] People were healed by arranging for the shadow of Peter to fall on them.[47] People brought scarves and other articles of clothing for Paul to touch so that the owners would be healed.[48] When they brought a lame man to Jesus on a mat, he ordered him to take up his bed and walk, and he did.[49] Peter did the same.[50]

At a certain point in Jesus' career, he set his face steadfast to go to Jerusalem, where he expected to be killed.[51] Paul, likewise set his face steadfast to go to Jerusalem and Rome, realizing that he would not return to see the people to whom he said, "Fare-well."[52] Jesus appeared before the Roman governor, Pilate, who found no guilt worthy of death.[53] Paul appeared before the Roman governor, Festus, who found Paul had done nothing worthy of death.[54] Both were under accusation of the Jews.

These statements reflect more doctrine than factual history. The narrator, who believed Jesus had ordained these apostles to be his agents reasoned that they must have done the things Jesus did, since an agent acts in behalf of a principal and in his name. In this conviction, he composed examples of Jesus' actions and goals being fulfilled through the agency of the apostles.

Captivity Type. Even if Daube were not correct in his argument that the Exodus narrative itself was composed in terms of a captive/release pattern, it is certain that later diaspora experiences were interpreted as captivities or prison terms and were consistently understood in terms of debtor slavery. The earliest analysis of a second captivity is reflected in the Isaianic apocalypse. This was probably written nearly fifty years after the Assyrian captivity (722 B.C.), i.e. about 685-75 B.C., because the author expected a great trumpet blast, as at Jubilee, and thought at that time

all of the diaspora Israelites from Egypt and Assyria
would return the way debtor slaves were to return at
Jubilee.[55] This means the people taken captive into
Assyria were understood by that time to have been
debtor slaves, serving out a prescribed term until the
first Jubilee arrived, when all debtor slaves were to
be sent home, and all land taken to pay off debts
would be returned.[56]

The Deuteronomist had made that deduction sometime after the Assyrian captivity. It is unlikely that
he dreamed of a future exile out of a clear blue sky.
He probably interpreted an event that had already tak-
en place. After there had been a deportation of the
leaders of North Israel to Assyria, the Deuteronomist
"predicted" that it would take place, and explained
why the Lord let it happen.[57] Also, like the author of
the Isaianic apocalypse, the Deuteronomist promised
that the Lord would restore them to the land, as he
had done before when they were exiled in Egypt.[58] By
the time of Jeremiah, that prophet had at his disposal
both the "prophecies" of Deuteronomy and the history
of the North Israelite exile as bases for his prophecies that Judah also would be taken into exile. He had
only to pay attention to the international events of
his time to be able to predict that they would go to
Babylon rather than Assyria.

Many years later, after the Romans had taken
complete control of Herod's kingdom, deposed and
exiled his son, Archelaus, and organized a Roman taxa-
tion of Palestine (ca. A.D. 6/7), Zadok the Pharisee
and Judas of Galilee led a revolt against Rome. They
argued that the Romans had taken away their freedom,
and they considered themselves to be slaves and captives again. This thought continued, and it was the
basis of the great Roman-Jewish war of A.D. 66-72.
With the typology of the Exodus captivity in Egypt and
Babylon was also associated the hope of the Exodus release.

Exodus Typology. The earliest repetition of an exodus
type in biblical account is the leadership of Joshua,
the first successor to Moses. Just as Moses had sent
messengers in to spy out the land, so Joshua sent messengers in to spy out the land.[59] Just as the Lord
opened up the waters of the Red Sea to allow the Israelites to cross under the leadership of Moses, so
Joshua divided the waters of the Jordan so that the
Israelites could cross over on dry land.[60] Just as the
Lord commanded Moses to take off his shoes because he

was standing on holy ground, so Joshua was commanded to remove his shoes, because he was standing on holy ground.[61] Just as Moses gave a farewell address before he died, so Joshua gave a farewell address before he died.[62] Just as Moses called the Israelites to make a contract with the Lord, so Joshua invited the Israelites to make a contract with the Lord.[63] The author of Joshua not only presented the crossing of the Jordan as an antitype of the exodus from Egypt, but he pictured Joshua as a new Moses. The entire Exodus experience, with its theological interpretation, continued to be a type upon which later events were understood as antitypes.

Just as the Babylonian and later diaspora experiences were interpreted as captivity and as prison terms served by debtor slaves according to the Egyptian pattern, so the expectation of a new exodus from Babylon was understood as a logical consequence. The Isaianic apocalypse predicted a Jubilee trumpet to announce liberty to the captives of Assyria and Egypt. Jeremiah had followed Deuteronomic logic and "prophecy" in predicting the captivity because Jews had not really let their brothers go free on years of release.[64] He said the Lord would then fulfill the curses of the contract by giving the Jews a new type of "freedom"--freedom to the sword, pestilence, and famine.[65] When the Lord sent the Jews into Babylon, Jeremiah argued that they would have to work off their indebtedness to the Lord at half wages, just as the law decreed. This meant paying double for all of their sins.[66]

When the author of Second Isaiah realized that Cyrus was willing to cooperate with Jews in overthrowing the Babylonians and allowing Jews to return to Palestine, he observed that the Jubilee was at hand, so he announced release to the Babylonian captives.[67] He reasoned that if Cyrus was about to liberate them, it must be that Jews had already paid double for all their sins,[68] but even if they had not, they could be restored to the land according to debtor slave/release terms[69] because of the laws related to Jubilee. Second Isaiah anticipated a new exodus, patterned after the exodus from Egypt.

Instead of imagining that the Babylonian Jews would go back to Palestine by the same route they took to get there, going north-west through the Tigris-Euphrates valleys and then turning south through the Esdraelon Pass, he followed the Exodus from Egypt typo-

logy and visualized a new road being built from Babylon to Jerusalem, through the desert, because the Hebrews had traveled through a desert years before. He
also expected the same kind of provisions as before--
plenty of food and water, miracles of healing, and
freedom from ritualistic pollution.[70] Just as the Lord
had brought the Hebrews out on eagles' wings to establish them in their destined portion,[71] so the Jews of
Babylon would mount up on wings as eagles.[72]

As the Lord guided the Hebrews through the Red
Sea to escape from the Egyptians,[73] so he would again
lead the chosen people through the waters.[74] Just as
the Lord had sent his angel before the Hebrews as a
pillar of fire by night and a pillar of cloud by day
and followed them across the Red Sea in the same
way,[75] so Jews would return with the Lord before them
and behind them.[76] Just as the Lord drove away all of
Israel's enemies, showing himself to be the "man of
war,"[77] so Second Isaiah referred to the Lord as a
"man of wars"[78] who would prevail against the enemies
of the Jews.[79] These are only a few of the many Exodus
themes echoed by the Babylonian typologist.[80]

When Mark Anthony overpowered Gaius Cassius in
war (41 B.C.), the Jewish high priest, Hyrcanus, sent
an embassy to him, asking that he write to all of the
provincial governors to demand that Jews taken prison-
er by Cassius, contrary to the rules of war, be set
free.[81] This embassy probably couched the request in
terms of biblical liberation of debtor slaves, because
the letters sent to the various governors read like
this one to the people of Tyre: ". . . and whatever
was sold belonging to the Jews, whether people or
property, must be given back. The people [who have
been enslaved] are to be set free, as they were initially, and the property, restored to the original owners."[82] The rules of war to which the Jews appealed
apparently were the Levitical rules of Jubilee when
the slaves were to be set free and the property restored to its original owners.[83]

The author of Hebrews told his readers that
they then were in the very positions of the Hebrews
who escaped from Egypt and were in the wilderness at
the border of the promised land. Jesus had brought
about the forgiveness of all of their former sins, and
they had been liberated to enter the promised land and
their promised rest. At that point the wilderness gen-
eration rebelled, sent spies, and provoked the Lord,

and never entered their "rest." They wandered in the wilderness; they died there; and the promise of rest was never fulfilled. The author warned Christians that if they were disobedient, they would also be turned away, so he told them not to be at all disobedient or unfaithful.[84] The exodus type that was first patterned after the rules for Sabbath and Jubilee release continued as a basis for interpreting the contemporary situations Jews and Christians faced.[85]

The religious leaders who related their own periods of history to earlier periods and identified later leaders with earlier ones were not doing this for the purpose of writing novels. For them this was a serious endeavor. The Jew who created the new Joseph character and the one who anticipated a new Phinehas were not just playing games. The one expected a wise man like Daniel in the Babylonian captivity because there had been one in the Egyptian captivity. The other expected a new teacher of righteousness in a time of sinfulness because there had been one before in the time of great sinfulness. The Christian author who wrote Acts thought Jesus was the new Joshua and the apostles were the new judges who were fulfilling the commandments of Jesus with full legal authority and identification.

Jeremiah believed he was quoting the word of the Lord when he quoted Deuteronomy, and he thought the Jews were repeating the captivity type which the North Israelites had recently experienced. By the same token, both he and Second Isaiah believed the captivity was only a prelude to another antitype of the Egyptian Exodus.

Typologies were created when scholars, who were well acquainted with the earlier history of their nation, noticed a close relationship between their own period and an earlier one, between two earlier periods, or two individuals living in two different periods. The author of Daniel noticed that there had been two captivities before his time, so he conjectured a wise man to go with the second just like there had really been in the first--or, he may even have believed so fully that types recurred that he concluded there really must have been such a personality as a new Joseph who was an antitype of the real Joseph of Egypt. We can only guess about things like this. The medieval author thought he lived in a sinful period just like that of the mingling Israelites in the wilderness, so he anticipated a new Phinehas who would deliver the medieval Jews, just as Phinehas had done for the Isra-

12

elites in the wilderness. It seemed reasonable for these authors to expect ancient figures to reappear, because they thought time was cyclical, and that which had happened before would happen again.[86] Once ancient concepts are known, ancient logic seems reasonable, but typology is one of those concepts that has not always persuaded Western scholars.

PROBLEMS WITH TYPOLOGY

Ups and Downs. Typology has had a checker-board career across the centuries. On the one hand it has been recognized by scholars, because it clearly existed and was employed both in the HS (Hebrew Scripture) and in the NT (New Testament). It was also used by the apostolic fathers, the church fathers, and other church leaders up to the nineteenth century. On the other hand, it could easily be abused, and it was. Correspondences were forced that did not exist, and it was easily mingled with allegory and sometimes offered the same difficulties. Abuses and difficulties were not just those introduced by later Christian scholars, such as Luther and Calvin; they were used at a very early stage by the apostolic fathers themselves, and perhaps even in the scriptures.

Early Examples. Barnabas said Jesus was a typos of Isaac who was offered at the altar;[87] he was also a typos of the goat that bore the sins of the people on the Day of Atonement. Barnabas included as many detailed similarities as he could muster: people spat on both, cursed both, goaded both; both were destined to die. Even the scarlet wool that was put between the goat's horns was a typos of Jesus, placed in the church, "because whoever wished to take away the scarlet wool must suffer much because the thorns are terrible."[88]

Jesus was also a typos of the red heifer offered for the forgiveness of sins: The sticks used for fire are a typos of the cross; the sinful men who brought the heifer are like those who brought Jesus to be slain; the three boys who sprinkled ashes are like the three patriarchs, Abraham, Isaac, and Jacob.[89] When Moses stretched out his hands and raised them above all the people when they were fighting so that they could win the battle, this was a typos of the cross with Jesus' hands stretched out; the cross was also the fulfillment of the scripture, "All day long I stretched out my hands to a disobedient people."[90] Also the graven image of a serpent which Moses made and

13

put up on a place of honor so that people could receive healing was a _typos_ of Jesus on the cross.[91] Joshua (=Jesus), son of Nun, was also a _typos_ of Jesus, because as Moses commissioned Joshua to destroy the whole house of Amalek, so Jesus, as God's son, was to shatter the strength of kings.[92]

Rationalism. Origen and other church fathers were even more fantastic than this in their imaginary interpretations and their confusion of typology with allegory. These excesses continued through the time of the Reformers. Luther inaugurated a typological interpretation of the HS, and Calvin created a whole tradition of typological interpretation. All of this, however, came to an end with rationalism.[93] In the eighteenth century, many scholars stopped thinking about the Bible as a unit. They recognized divisions in the literature and began to analyze the different kinds of literature in the Bible and to compare them with other ancient Near Eastern literature. The NT was distinguished from the HS, and scholars like Harnack wished Luther had omitted the HS from the canon. When Christians accepted the HS they made Christianity a syncretistic religion, in Harnack's judgment, instead of becoming a pure religion.[94] These scholars did not study this literature as material for religious guidance. They called the HS "Mosaism" and studied it as the history of the religion of the HS the way they studied the religious literature of other religions. Since NT scholars read only the NT, there no longer was any motivation to notice any correspondences between the HS and the NT. At this point typology was exchanged for another kind of analogical thinking, the historical-critical method of biblical research.[95]

SCHOLARLY ANALYSES

Fairbairn. Typology was not dropped completely without any resistance. In the nineteenth century, Fairbairn published his extensive study in two large volumes.[96] There he attempted to answer and acknowledge the many problems involved in the use of typology as a method of biblical interpretation, but he also tried to establish some regulations and definitions that would allow the phenomenon to continue as a contemporary discipline. He said, "If the Typology of Scripture cannot be rescued from the domain of allegorizings, it will be impossible to secure for it a solid and permanent footing."[97] There were other problems, however, that Fairbairn did not notice. He presumed that the typological interpretations of the HS given in the NT were the true interpretations of the HS and showed the divine intent God had in the beginning.

14

<u>Trench</u>. Trench shared similar views. He said that the type and antitype inherently belonged together. They were not just drawn together by accident but by inward necessity. The law of a secret affinity had destined them to be together long before.[98] These were not adequate answers for the skeptics, so typology was largely discredited among biblical scholars. Semler said of typology, "He who assumes no types . . . is deprived of nothing whatever."[99] Many of the objections made were legitimate, and the attitude of skepticism continued until after the first World War.

<u>Westermann</u>. In his account of the development of biblical studies after World War 1, Westermann said, "Now something very strange happened: The very foundation upon which the concept of history of religions had developed and which had been the basis of the theological work of the teachers and scholars of this school began to be shaken."[100] Scholars began to ask themselves if they were only historians. Were they dealing with anything worth dying for? It was Rudolph Kittel who first confronted scholars with this problem.[101] Then began a Neo-Orthodoxy movement which became stronger after World War 2. HS scholars began to study the HS theologically. At the same time they started to speak of God's revealing himself in the history of Israel, of God as the God who lives in history and acts in history, and of the HS as the history of God with his people. Biblical theology was thought of as a confessional recital of God's redemptive acts in history.[102]

With this movement came an interest in the Bible as a unit. This was not just a reversion to the precritical period of biblical study, but it changed the attitude of scholars toward the literature. The new reexamination of the Bible began to reattract scholars to typology--that which had been discredited long before. Scholars who began to reexamine typology did so cautiously, but there were still some of the same mistakes that discredited typology originally. Most admitted problems, proceeded rather slowly, and tried to redefine typology and distinguish it from allegory. The biggest mistake made was that of accepting the NT interpretation of the HS type as the valid intentional and true meaning even of the HS type. Another was that of confusing literary analysis with theology. Some of the first to undertake this project were Danielou, Vischer, Eichrodt, Von Rad, and Goppelt.[103]

Danielou. Danielou set out to show how typology was employed by the church fathers, but he introduced his subject by showing that typology was used in the HS itself and in the Jewish intertestamental literature before the fathers began their task.[104] Following Irenaeus, Danielou said, "Typology here is the mouthpiece of theology: the dogma of Christ as the new Adam, and of Mary's mediation rests on the typological significance of the Genesis account. To dispute this typology would be to go against the whole of ecclesiastical tradition."[105] St. Chrysostom said the relationship of the type with the antitype was such that you could see the superiority of the latter over the former. If the type had nothing in common with the anti-type, then there would be nothing typical. On the other hand, it was not necessary for one to be identical to the other. If that were the case, the antitype would be the type itself. There must be a proportion. "Do not expect the Old Testament to explain everything, but even if you do find certain mysteries (ainigmata) which are difficult and obscure, learn how to be satisfied."[106]

Danielou organized his study around such figures as Adam, Noah, Isaac, Moses, Joshua, and Rahab. Church fathers found many typologies around Paradise, the Exodus from Egypt, the wilderness, and the entrance into the promised land. Nearly every situation around water became a type for Christian baptism--the flood, the Red Sea, the bitter waters, the water flowing from the rock after Moses struck it with his staff, and the crossing of the Jordan. Danielou said one of the reasons typology was important to the church fathers was that it furthered their attack against Marcion by showing the necessity of the HS. In his comparison of typology and prophecy, Danielou said, "The organic relation between typology and prophecy, typos and logos is quite clear, for so far from being distinct categories, prophecy is the typological interpretation of history."[107]

Vischer. Vischer reviewed the content of the Pentateuch and the earlier prophets to find biblical witnesses to the Christ or the Messiah. He said Jesus belongs to the NT but the Messiah belongs to the HS. It is necessary, then, to study the HS to learn the office of the Messiah that Jesus filled.[108] In Jesus Christ, then, the HS and NT come together into an integral unity. A person who disparages the HS cannot really be a Christian, in Vischer's judgment.[109] Vischer believed that God anticipated in these HS events s

16

the NT events that were still to come. For example in
Noah's flood, God anticipated the future judgment, in
Vischer's opinion.[110]

Eichrodt. Eichrodt said the antitype does not correspond to the type in all of its properties, but only
one or two details in which the author was interested.
For example, Moses and Christ correspond only on the
points of glory and ministry in 2 Cor. 3:7-4:6, but
types can also be contrasting, as in Adam and
Christ.[111] To avoid the problems of allegory, Eichrodt
said typology does not concentrate on details, but
"aims toward the center of the establishment of salvation by God. Thus it is Jesus Christ who provides in
the first place the antitype of the Old Testament
types." Besides Jesus there are also other antitypes,
but not of subordinate variety. They are all central
elements in the realization of salvation.[112] Type dif-
fers from prophecy in that it requires no human medium, and is often disclosed only when looking backward
from the NT time of salvation. Eichrodt called it a
kind of "objectivized prophecy" or "realized prophecy."[113] He also argued that typology was already
known in the HS itself in such types as the exodus,
David, the high priest, and the primeval prophet of
Deuteronomy 18:15.[114] He disagreed with those who objected to the use of NT typologies to clarify meanings
in the HS, saying that this is what distinguishes
Christian exegesis from Jewish exegesis.[115]

Irwin. Irwin took strong issue with Eichrodt on this
last point. Irwin said, "If Eichrodt wishes to introduce typology as a department of Christian dogmatics,
well and good; that is an issue for the dogmatists;
he, or anyone else so disposed, has yet to show that
it belongs to biblical research."[116] It was not typology per se to which Irwin objected. He responded to it
at the same time he reacted against the way it was
used. He opposed the infusion of a theological point
of view into the text from the outside. He thought typology might be all right for NT exgesis, but from the
perspective of HS insights it was not hermeneutic but
homiletic. The historian should not be influenced by
his confession of faith in an objective analysis of a
HS text.[117] Jewish scholars strongly approved Irwin's
stance. Although they acknowledged that typology
existed, they objected to it being used as if Judaism
were only a preparatory type for which Christianity
was the more advanced antitype. Irwin was mostly correct, and others[118] have concurred that typology
should not be confused with exegesis, but even in the

HS typology exists, and the exegete cannot fairly ignore it. For example, when examining a text in Hosea which deals with the wilderness experience typologically, recognition of this fact is important for the exegesis of Hosea, although not for the exegesis of Exodus, Numbers, or Deuteronomy.

Baumgaertel. Without mentioning Eichrodt's name, Baumgaertel emphasized the same point as Irwin. He said people in the HS had a different point of view from either those of the NT or of people today. A pious Christian may have a meaningful, but erroneous, understanding of an HS text. In order to understand the HS text fairly the scholar must divorce himself or herself, mentally and emotionally, from his or her contemporary point of view as well as his or her Christian position based on the NT. Only then can he or she see the HS text fairly. The scholar can then learn from the NT the point of view of the NT leaders about this text, but this will not be the same as the meaning of the text in its own time. A third step is to understand the various subjective views of contemporary Christians about both texts. Baumgaertel only mentioned typology in passing, because it seemed to be one of the tools used by modern Christians to misunderstand both the HS and the NT. He did not mention Eichrodt at all, but Eichrodt understood that he was an object of Baumgaertel's attack. Eichrodt, however, responded with only an apologetic confession of faith.[119]

Irwin and Baumgaertel both offered just criticisms. Since typology was reintroduced into biblical scholarship at the same time and by the same people who were active in the new emphasis on theology, it is not surprising that typology became one of the tools that was abused by interpreting HS texts on the basis of their NT antitype and both by current antitypes. This was associated with Existentialism and the "new hermeneutic," whose practice was to learn what the scripture meant for us today. This does not mean that typology cannot be understood fairly as it was actually used in the HS (Hebrew Scripture) and the NT. In fact Wolff argued that typology was historically based, had its origin in the Bible, and was still valid in the twentieth century.[120] Goppelt said it is the predominant method in the NT and characteristic of it.[121] Others have concurred in these judgments.

Von Rad. Von Rad tried to correct some of Eichrodt's errors. He said typological thinking was not specifically a theological point of view or a peculiarly Oriental way of thinking, but it was "an elementary function of all human thought and interpretation."[122] Although many countries have analogies between heavenly prototypes and earthly types, the HS is dominated by a typological thinking that involves eschatology--the beginning and the end, the return to paradise,[123] the return to a pristine David,[124] the wilderness days,[125] and the Davidic Jerusalem.[126] He warned against the pitfall of theologians thinking they must use typology to draw some special meaning or ideology from texts.[127]

In defining the new role of typology, Von Rad listed the following characteristics: 1) It is a fundamental way of historical understanding of the HS texts. 2) It has to do with the entire HS. 3) It related only to the divine event. It does not fix upon historical details. 4) Typological interpretation is aware of the difference between the HS and the NT. 5) It transcends self-understanding of the HS text, but it is not sharply separated from the historico-critical exegetical process. 6) There is no pedagogical norm that can be set up to apply to all typological cases. 7) Current typology is so different and so much more complicated than formerly, Von Rad wondered if another word should be used for this new discipline.[128] After examining numerous possibilities, scholars like Baker and Davidson finally concluded that typology was the legitimate word to use for this phenomenon. It needs only to be properly defined and used.

Goppelt. After reviewing typology in other Jewish literature, Goppelt set out to make a thorough study of typology in the NT. He first studied the typology of the gospels related to Jesus under titles of prophet, son of David, Lord, and Son of man. Then in the gospels and Acts, he examined typologies of the church, first as the calling of the twelve tribes, second as people of the new contract, third, the church of Pentecost, fourth, as the new creation, fifth as the children of Abraham, and sixth, as the spiritual Israel. Goppelt turned from the church to typology in Hebrews, with Jesus as the heavenly high priest. After Hebrews, he studied the Fourth Gospel, where he found Jesus typifying the perfecter of creation and the perfect gift.

Some of his conclusions are as follows: 1) "The typology in the Synoptic Gospels is usually a simple

19

reminder of the HS parallels by means of the names
that are given to NT phenomena or by allusions that
are included in the narrative";[129] 2) "[t]he relationship in redemptive history is taken for granted by the
evangelists and the rest of the NT because they are
convinced that there is a continuity between HS history and Jesus Christ in the sense of preparation and
fulfillment";[130] 3) "in Paul and in Hebrews[,] [t]ype
and antitype are explicitly compared; the common elements and the heightening are emphasized, and prophecy
is used to indicate how they are related to each
other";[131] 4) "typology is the method of exegesis that
is the characteristic use of Scripture in the NT. Typology is found in only a small portion of contemporary Judaism's usage of Scripture and solely in the
development of its eschatology";[132] 5) "[t]ypology begins and ends with the present salvation. NT typology
is not trying to find the meaning of some HS story or
institution";[133] and 6) "typology is not a hermeneutical method with specific rules of interpretation. It
is a spiritual approach that looks forward to the consummation of salvation and recognizes the individual
types of that consummation in redemptive history."[134]
The three certainties Goppelt considered his research
to prove are these: "(1) Typology is unknown in the
nonbiblical Hellenist environment of early Christianity. (2) It is found exclusively in the Jewish environment, but only as a principle of eschatology. (3)
The typology that is found in Judaism had a prior history in the eschatology of the HS."[135]

Baker. In his attempt to define typology, Baker said
it was not exegesis, prophecy, allegory, symbolism, or
any method or system. Although the church fathers developed an elaborate system, the Bible gives no list
of types and it offers no elaborate method of interpretation.[136] He also disagreed with some of the qual-
ifications given by others: He thought the idea that
it had to be designed by God was not helpful. Furthermore, he thought any set of rules to be provided arbi-
trarily for use in the Bible was not fair. Those who
limited it to something concerned with God's redemptive activity did not offer anything meaningful. There
were many redemptive themes in the Bible, but there
were others, like the Kingdom of God, which had typical aspects. In response to the suggestion that types
must always point to something future, Baker said that
it was only in retrospect from the corresponding antitype that a type could be recognized. Also, Baker said
there was no necessary progression or increase from
type to antitype. They could move either from more to
less or less to more.[137]

On the positive side, Baker insisted that typology is historical, concerned with historical facts and not words. There must also be a real correspondence and not only an agreement of detail. As examples of trivial details, he thought the correspondences found by the church fathers between Rahab's scarlet thread and the death of Christ and the relationship between the ax head that floated for Elisha and the cross of Christ were strained.[138] There can be no doubt about Baker's judgment, but it is also necessary to deal with facts. If the church fathers called these trivial details typology, then it was typology for them. If authors of the NT also made trivial correspondences, then this should be recognized, even if Westerners do not find it sufficiently systematic to suit us.

DAVIDSON'S WORD STUDIES

NT Usages. There have been numerous articles, books, and critical book reviews on the topic of typology,[139] but prior to Davidson's work, no one had made a complete word-study of the use of Typos in its various forms in the Bible. Since definitions and interpretations of this discipline varied and the consequent opinions of typology differed accordingly, Davidson set out to examine every use of the term in the NT in order to find a firm base for describing this phenomenon.[140] He quickly learned that the noun typos occurs fifteen times in the NT: most of these usages are in the letters of Paul. The term occurs three times in Acts, twice in John and once each in Hebrews and 1 Peter. The noun-adjective antitypos occurs once in Hebrews and once in First Peter. The adverb typikôs appears only in First Corinthians 10:11, and the noun hypotyposis was used twice.[141]

NT Meanings. In John 20:25 the terms seems to mean "mark," or "print." Typos in Acts 7:42-44 means "idol," "graven image," "model," or "pattern."[142] The reference in Acts 23:25 seems to mean "text" or "message" of a letter.[143] The type of teaching,[144] Davidson concludes is something concrete, derived, and normative and has the power to stamp and mold those committed to it.[145] Sometimes typos is a pattern or model of "walking."[146] In this case, the ultimate model is Christ, who acts as the "typer" or "molder" for Paul, who, in turn, became a model or type for Christian leaders to imitate.[147] The same ethical meaning is required of First Thessalonians 1:7 with the leaders acting as models or patterns for other believers.

Davidson argued that the word "example" does not
do the context justice, since the type here was
stamped by Paul and the leaders would also be stampers
for other Christians. It was more than an influence;
it was a predestined and precast form.[148] The same is
true of its use in Second Thessalonians 3:9, First
Timothy 4:12, and Titus 2:7. Hypotyposis probably refers to a prototype, outline, or rough sketch for further work.[149] Davidson observed that all of these were
ethical terms, but they involved more than being good
moral examples. It was a set, determined model with
specific requirements. The translations given in most
New Testaments do not reflect the force of a type that
fits a corresponding type, prototype, or antitype.[150]
These involve specific ethics and practices of a determined content that are passed on without change.
That which Paul received from Christ was passed on to
church leaders who then passed it on to other church
members.

TYPOLOGICAL HERMENEUTICS

1 Cor 10:1-13. Among the usages of typos in the NT,
there were six that belong to a structure in which the
author was interpreting a specific passage of HS
scripture. Davidson examined these with care, beginning with First Corinthians 10:1-13:

> I do not want you to be ignorant, brothers, [of
> the fact] that our fathers were all under the
> cloud, and all went through the [Red] Sea. All
> were baptized in the cloud and in the sea; all
> ate of the same spiritual food; all drank of
> the same spiritual drink, for they were drink-
> ing from the spiritual rock which followed, and
> the rock was the Messiah. But with most of them
> God was not pleased, for they were scattered in
> the wilderness (Num 14:16, 22, 30).

> Now, these things became types of us, so that
> you might not be lusters (Num 11:4, 34) of
> evil, just as those [Israelites] lusted, and do
> not become idolaters, as some of them were, as
> it is written, the people sat down, ate, drank,
> and stood up to play (Num 23:1, 9). Let us not
> commit sexually improper acts as some of them
> behaved sexually improperly, and twenty-three
> thousand of them fell in one day, and neither
> let us tempt the Lord, just as some of them
> tempted, and they were destroyed by serpents.

22

Do not complain, as some of them grumbled, and they were destroyed by the destroyer.

These things happened to those [Israelites], but it was written as our warning, [us] to whom the ends of the ages have come, so that the one who thinks he stands, let him watch so that he does not fall. Temptation has not taken you that is not humanly [normal], but God is faithful, who will not permit you to be tempted beyond that which you are able [to endure], but he will make with the temptation also the outcome so that [you] will be able to bear [it].

This passage consists of historical narrative and exhortation. Paul first described and interpreted things that had happened to the Israelites in the wilderness. Then he warned the Corinthians that they were in the same predicament and that if they did not behave differently from the way their fathers had, they would also suffer the same evil consequences. In the two cases in which Paul interrupted his narrative, he said "these things" were either typoi or typikôs. This makes this an excellent example for studying the meaning of NT typology, as Davidson realized.

Following an examination of the passage for integrity, Davidson was convinced that this was a unit and genuinely Pauline, and that Paul was interpreting the Exodus passage. Davidson noted that Paul's use of the expression, "our fathers," meaning the Hebrew patriarchs, was extended to mean that all Christians, Jews and Gentiles alike, were included as members of the same heritage. Like the Corinthians, the early Israelites had been baptized, received blessings, ate and drank at feasts, and received divine protection. Israelites had been baptized into Moses as Christians had been baptized into Christ.[151]

Davidson observed that Paul was comparing two historical events that involved the formation of two communities, their initiation, and deliverance, and although both participated in sacraments, these were not guarantees that God would be pleased. The rock that Moses struck to provide water for the Israelites in the wilderness[152] went with them throughout their desert wanderings to provide water for them. This was the belief both of Paul and of later rabbis.[153] When Paul said that the rock that provided this water was Christ, Davidson thought he was identifying Christ with the angel that accompanied the Israelites. When

23

Paul said these things had become types (typoi) of Christians--not for Christians--Paul meant that they were the antitypes of which the Israelites were the types. The blessings the Israelites were offered provided positive or negative results, depending on the response of the Israelites. The Corinthian Christians were in the same position. They also could be scattered and destroyed in plagues just as was the lot of most of the Israelites. Paul used this historical event as a warning to the Christians. The events that happened to their fathers were given as types of what was destined to happen to the Corinthians if they acted in the same way. All of these things really happened, and the reason they happened was to show the Christians what to do and what not to do. Types were related here to purpose, both in 10:6 and 10:11:

> "(vs. 6):
> A. (nature) These things became types of us,
> B. (purpose) so that we might not become lusters of evil . . .
>
> (vs. 11):
> A. (nature) Now these things happened to them typically,
> B. (purpose) and were written as a warning for us."[154]

One of the important insights anyone gets as he or she examines this text is that Paul's consideration of the type was not just a general outline; nor was it limited to the central point. Paul examined it in great detail and showed the Corinthians point-by-point similarities between their behavior and that of the Israelites in the wilderness. These are not as trivial as those of Barnabas or Origen, but they are detailed, and they are Pauline.[155] These are objective facts about NT typology that cannot be ruled out by anyone who happens not to like typology as a methodology.

Davidson correctly noted that Paul believed that the reports of the Exodus and wilderness events were historical events and those of the Corinthians were also historical. Furthermore, Paul was working with a Hebrew Scripture text. This was his typological method of exegesis.[156] Paul was not comparing symbols or philosophical ideas. There was a horizontal relationship between the Hebrew Scripture type and the Corinthian antitype, and Paul described them in terms of the Greek typos and typikôs.

24

Romans 5:12-21. Another detailed Pauline exegesis of a
Hebrew Scripture passage is in Romans:

> Because of this, just as through one man, sin
> entered the world, and through sin, death, and
> thus death entered through all human beings,
> for all sinned. Before the law sin was in the
> world, but sin was not reckoned, since there
> was no law [defining it]. But death ruled from
> Adam until Moses over those who had not sinned
> following the transgression of Adam, who was a
> type of the coming one. Not as the transgres-
> sion, however, was the grace. For if by means
> of the transgression of the one, the many died,
> how much more the grace of God and the gift by
> means of grace of the one man Jesus the Messiah
> has overflowed to the many. Not as through the
> one, having sinned, is the gift. On the one
> hand the judgment of the one [transgression] is
> conviction, but, on the other hand, the gift
> from many transgressions is acquittal, for if
> by means of the transgression of the one, death
> ruled through the one man, how much more those
> who have received the overflow of grace and the
> gift of a [judgment of] acquittal will rule in
> life through the one man, Jesus the Messiah.
> Therefore then, just as through the transgres-
> sion of one man [the verdict goes] to all human
> beings for condemnation, thus also through the
> righteousness of one man [the verdict goes] to
> all men for acquittal of life, for just as
> through the disobedience of the one man the
> many were established sinners, thus also
> through the obedience of the one man the many
> were established innocent, for the law entered
> so that the trespass might increase, but where
> sin increased grace increased excessively, so
> that just as sin ruled by means of death, thus
> also grace ruled through righteousness to life
> of the age through Jesus, the Messiah, our
> Lord.

This passage includes much repetition and rhetorical logic, but it dealt with Adam as if he had
been a historical personage and not just a philosophical personification of the human race. He was also reported in the Hebrew Scriptures, so Paul was expounding on a text, typologically. For Paul, Adam was the
type and Christ was the antitype. Since by Paul's time
the existence of both was past history, Paul had been
able to interpret the relationship between the two,

and he did this typologically. Paul did not invent typology for this occasion, but he used a method of interpretation of scripture that was just as familiar to
him as the a fortiori arguments he used at the same
time, and he used the word typos to describe the figure that was historically prior to the "coming one,"
who would have been the antitype.

1 Peter 3:18-22.
> Christ died once for sins, an innocent man in
> behalf of guilty people, in order that you
> might approach God, on the one hand, having
> died to the flesh, but on the other hand, hav-
> ing been made alive in the spirit inasmuch as
> he went and preached to the spirits in prison,
> who at one time were disobedient when the long
> suffering of God waited in the days of Noah,
> while the ark was being prepared, into which a
> few, i.e. eight people, were saved through wa-
> ter--which antitype, baptism now saves you, not
> from the removal of fleshly filth, but an ap-
> peal to God for a good conscience through the
> resurrection of Jesus the Messiah.

This passage is important, because it is not
Pauline. It shows that the concept of type and antitype were well-known types of exegesis in New Testament times. The author of this document used the term
"antitype," for baptism as an antitype for water of
Noah, which was the type, but the typology really included more items than one. On the one side were
placed the water, the eight who had been saved, and
Noah, whereas on the other side were baptism, Christians who had been saved, and Christ. Like Paul, the
author of First Peter thought of Noah as an actual
historical figure who lived and built an ark. Likewise
Jesus was an actual person who lived and died in behalf of others. The relationship between these two was
considered typologically.

SUMMARY

After these three illustrations, it is no longer reasonable to question the existence of typology
as a method of hermeneutics used in New Testament
times. Both Paul and the author of First Peter used
it, employing terms like typos, typikôs, and antitypos coherently. All three examples were applied to
historical figures in biblical history. There are
others that apply perpendicularly, in Platonic fashion, with the prototype in heaven and the corres-

26

ponding type on earth, but it is important to show that NT authors used this method hermeneutically. Farrer correctly said typology is not a hypothesis; it is a fact. The same is true of allegory. Scholars are free to argue about whether or not typology and allegory are legitimate ways to reason and interpret texts, but there can be no question about the historical fact that both were employed in New Testament times. When Paul and the author of First Peter used typology in exegesis, they did not conform to twentieth century scholars' definition of typology in terms of general comparisons alone. They related the antitype to the type at as many detailed points as they could. They were not as trivial as the points later church fathers used in the name of typology, but they were detailed.

Anyone who spends hours and years reading exegesis composed by church fathers, rabbis, or other doctrinally oriented exegetes will not be surprised to find some fantastic or trivial points in the arguments. These pious authors were not scientists or analysts but dogmatists, writing for other apologists of the same convictions. Some of their logic was amazingly creative, even if it would not seem logical to Western minds. Their arguments were accepted, because no one wanted to disagree. All of these exegetes used typology as one method of interpretation. It was consistent with their belief that time moved in cycles, so that events, institutions, and characters at identical points in earlier and later cycles could be compared typologically, because, to some extent, they were identical. This will be more evident after an examination of cyclical time in antiquity.

TIME AND CYCLES

Josephus. After Josephus had described the destruction of Jerusalem in A.D. 70, he marvelled at the exactness of the cycle of destiny which predestined the temple to burn at the hands of the Romans on the very month and day on which it was burned by the Babylonians, years before the second fall.[157] Josephus's easy allusion to cycles was no isolated example, completely removed from normal Hebrew and Jewish thought.

Not only Jews and Christians, but other peoples, like Greeks, Egyptians, Mayas, and Aztecs thought time moved in cycles.[158] It was normal for agricultural peoples to think this way. One day came to an end only to have another begin. The same was true of weeks, years, sabbath years, and jubilee years.

27

Seasons moved in a predestined order: like night and day, there was winter and summer every year. Annual feasts were associated with exactly the same seasons every year. People's lives were governed by the reliability of these cycles, so the philosophical members of such societies as these deduced further that in some way longer periods of time, such as ages, also succeeded each other the way day followed night, and they tried to associate these ages so as to be able to predict the events of one on the basis of its predecessor. Evidence of this way of thinking is not hard to find.

Scripture and Scrolls. In the HS itself, the Koheleth held that the events in time circled like the wind, so that the events that happened currently had already happened before and would happen again.[159] "The Psalm of the Seasons" in the Community Rule took both cycles and seasons for granted and considered them all occasions for praise to God. Just as part of each day was ruled by the day and another part by the night, so the children of light (Jews) ruled part of the time and children of darkness (Gentiles) ruled the rest of the time. These rules were predestined to alternate just as regularly as day and night.[160] The Sibyl narrated history in terms of cycles of times, cycles of seasons, and cycles of years.[161]

Predestined Cycles. One ancient Jewish author reasoned, "God created all the Gentiles which are on the circle of the earth as well as us. He foresaw them and us from the beginning of creation of the circle of the earth until the departure of the age, and nothing has been neglected by him even to minute details, but everything he foresaw, and he moved everything forward as a whole."[162] The same Jewish prophet seemed to think that God predestined Jews and Gentiles to relate to each other across the ages of time. Second Baruch spelled this out more clearly. He said the time between Adam and the Messiah was divided into twelve periods of alternative good and bad fortune for Israel. These periods were probably considered twenty-four ages or twelve complete cycles of time.[163] On the basis of such predestined cycles of time the NT seer said the four messengers to be released from the Euphrates had been prepared there "for the hour and day and month and year."[164]

Second Isaiah. Anyone as convinced as these people were that time repeated itself was predisposed to look for signs of objects, people, or events that happened in their own time that matched earlier people, events, or objects and were therefore antitypes of earlier types. Some of their identifications were forced and subjective, reflecting more prejudice than objective deduction, but this is not a unique phenomenon in religious history. One of the more careful biblical typologists was Second Isaiah who recognized some signs in recent Jewish history that matched events that had occurred earlier.

Egyptian Cycle. Beginning with the captivity in Egypt, history continued for the Hebrews with their crossing the Red Sea, going into the wilderness, and there receiving provisions through miracles—water, meat, victory in war, and healing of diseases. This was followed by a conquest of the promised land, establishment of a kingdom, and construction of a temple at Jerusalem. Second Isaiah may even have noticed that the captivity in Egypt was for about four hundred years, and the period of "rest" under Davidic rule was for about four hundred years before the destruction of Jerusalem and the new captivity. From captivity to captivity—the cycle was complete. This period of history showed the beginning and end of two ages—one ruled by Gentiles and one ruled by Israelites. If he had put his concepts of earlier Hebrew history onto a graph, he may have drawn a circle something like this:

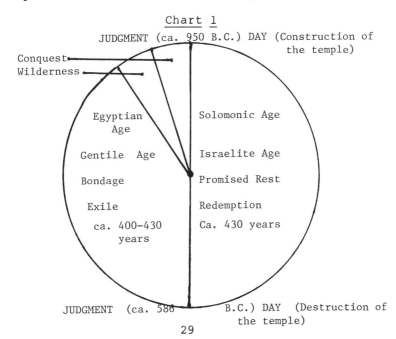

Chart 1

JUDGMENT (ca. 950 B.C.) DAY (Construction of the temple)

Conquest
Wilderness

Egyptian Age

Gentile Age

Bondage

Exile

ca. 400-430 years

Solomonic Age

Israelite Age

Promised Rest

Redemption

Ca. 430 years

JUDGMENT (ca. 586 B.C.) DAY (Destruction of the temple)

29

Babylonian Cycle. If Second Isaiah had drawn for himself any such sketches, they have not survived, but that is no disaster. If we could have only one, it is much better for us to have Second Isaiah's poetry than his sketches. We might be able to deduce graphs from poetry, but we could hardly compose Second Isaiah's poetry from graphs. If, however, he had diagrammed such a graph as the one above to visualize past history, he might easily have reconstructed another, on that basis, which would project the future graphic cycle--from captivity to captivity.

Chart 2

EXPECTED JUDGMENT DAY

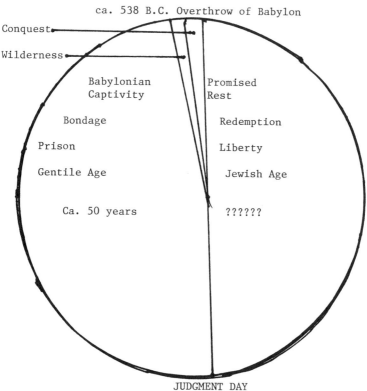

ca. 538 B.C. Overthrow of Babylon

Conquest

Wilderness

Babylonian Captivity

Promised Rest

Bondage

Redemption

Prison

Liberty

Gentile Age

Jewish Age

Ca. 50 years

??????

JUDGMENT DAY
Ca. 586 B.C. (Destruction of the Temple)

30

Some of the content of Second Isaiah's poetry
that enables us to deduce his cyclical typology is the
following: Just as the Lord's servant, Moses, enabled
Hebrews to escape from Egypt, the Lord would again
provide a servant to escape from Babylon.[165] At that
time the wilderness would blossom like a rose,[166] the
blind would receive their sight; deaf people would
hear; lame would walk.[167] This could be expected because Moses had healed Miriam in the wilderness before. As Moses provided water, miraculously, so there
would again be pools of water in the desert,[168] and
guidance for all those who returned through the wilderness to the promised land.[169] Since they had gone
through the sea before, so they would have to go
through the waters again.[170]

Ignored Obstacles. If the prophet had been absolutely
objective in his analysis and consistent in his conviction, he would have assumed Jews in Babylon were
destined for a four hundred year sentence, but he already knew of Jewish negotiations with Cyrus of Persia
who was prepared, with Jewish internal assistance, to
capture Babylon and release Jews to return to Palestine. With this in the offing, he presumed everything
had been accelerated. Instead of a four hundred year
captivity period, this one would be only about fifty.
The forty years' wilderness wandering would be paralleled by a wilderness crossing that would take only a
few days, as the Jews walked from Babylon to Jerusalem
on a newly built Garden State Parkway. Since there was
the political and military backing of Cyrus, he saw no
lengthy conquest. Jews would have authority to return
in broad daylight, and Cyrus had promised to finance
the venture. This was all miraculous, but orderly. It
conformed to the Egyptian cycle; it was the antitype
of the preceding age.

Hasmonean Cycle. When Persia conquered Babylon, and
Jewish life was restored in Palestine under the leadership of Zerubbabel and Joshua, it was not nearly as
glorious as Second Isaiah had visualized. Most Jews
did not think they were really back to the good old
days of David and Solomon, but at a much later date,
after the temple had been defiled and cleansed, and
Jews were beginning to regain the promised land, another cyclical typologist reinterpreted past history
so as to make it conform better with the previous cycle. After all, he had many points in his favor: About
422 years had elapsed since the beginning of the captivity, rather than 50. This corresponded much better
with the Egyptian captivity.

Furthermore, by his time the temple had actually been cleansed and dedicated--a repetition of the dedication of Solomon's temple! Therefore the author of Daniel interpreted the history from the destruction of the temple in 586 B.C. to the rededication in 164 B.C.--from temple to temple. He forced the facts a little to make it all come out in sabbaths as well as cycles, but that was permissible for dogmaticians. He was giving a religious interpretation to history that had already occurred. He was not trying to prophesy future history on the basis of the past. His Sabbath doctrine changed the captivity period from 422 years to 490 years, but he tried to do this inconspicuously. He concentrated on the first week of years in Babylon and the last week of years in Jerusalem. In between he forced sixty-two weeks of years, without balancing the totals. True to the dual period of wilderness and conquest, this eschatologist divided the final period into two half weeks of years: 1) from the treaty with Antiochus to the defilement of the temple, and 2) from the defilement of the temple to its cleansing. Had this theologian put his interpretation onto a cyclical graph, it might have looked something like this:

Chart 3

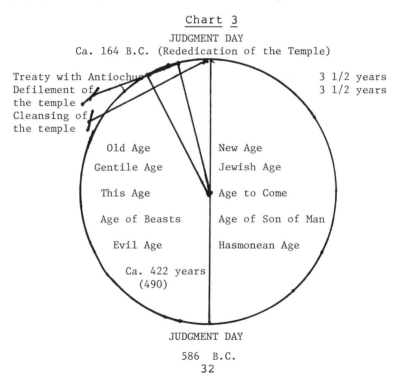

JUDGMENT DAY
Ca. 164 B.C. (Rededication of the Temple)

Treaty with Antiochus   3 1/2 years
Defilement of   3 1/2 years
the temple
Cleansing of
the temple

Old Age   New Age

Gentile Age   Jewish Age

This Age   Age to Come

Age of Beasts   Age of Son of Man

Evil Age   Hasmonean Age

Ca. 422 years
(490)

JUDGMENT DAY

586 B.C.

Roman Captivity. By NT times, the new Hasmonean Age, the beginning of which provided high expectations for the author of Daniel and other contemporary Jews who had shared in that famous Hanukkah celebration, had slowly collapsed. Pompey had reentered the temple; Herod's rule was strong, but very pro-Roman; Herod's sons could not control the nationalistic rebels, so Rome installed its own governors and tax collectors. Zealous Jews knew they were no longer free, and they began to reanalyze their past history to find out how long they would have to endure this Roman age before the Jewish age to come would be reinstituted. They looked for current antitypes of ancient types and current signs of the recurrence of ancient miracles. They were so eager for the new age to come that they forced almost any current event to be a clue to understanding their age. They did not want a sign that would say they were back at the beginning of the Egyptian period just after Joseph. They wanted signs to show that the wilderness period was just about over. This was the tenor of the times into which Jesus and John entered, saying, "The time is up; the Kingdom of Heaven is near." Jews understood this to mean the time of the Roman control over Palestine was over; and the Jewish kingdom was about to be reestablished at Jerusalem.

CONCLUSIONS

One of the major opponents to the modern revival of typology was Bultmann. Bultmann argued that typology depended upon an ancient oriental cyclical view of time,[171] and, without examining the possibility that Jews and Christians really understood time in cycles, he presumed that such a view was false. He was correct in his analysis that typology and cyclical time concepts belong together, but he was wrong in his assumption that cyclical time was foreign to biblical thought. It was because Jews and Christians thought of time as moving in cycles that they were motivated to study the signs of the times, relate the events of their time to the events of earlier cycles and identify current institutions, people, and events to corresponding institutions, people, and events of earlier times. The word, "type" was an appropriate term for characters that reappeared cycle after cycle and provided a basis for believing they would appear again for Christians to whom the ends of the ages had all coincided. It is clear now that neither typology nor a cyclical view of time are modern New Testament hypotheses; they are facts that existed in NT times. Hypoth-

eses and conjectures are involved in identifying some
of these, and some errors in conjecture undoubtedly
will be made, but they can be made on the basis of
facts of NT times.

Daube was correct in thinking that the exodus
pattern was the most important pattern of deliverance
in the Bible. Both Daube and Carmichael were right in
discovering typological methodologies in early composition of literature. Literary composers prepared
their documents with the invention or identification
of new antitypes of Joseph, Phinehas, Elijah, or Jesus. They identified their historical period with earlier times in Egypt, the wilderness, the conquest of
Canaan, or the dedication of the temple. The end which
they anticipated was the antitype of the end of the
captivity of Egypt or Babylon, and the kingdom for
which they longed was an antitype of the United Kingdom of David or Solomon. They strained their mental
resources to make these expectations fit into the
cyclical understanding of time that was standard for
that period of history in the Greco-Roman world.

Even after the crucifixion, Christian typologists continued to interpret the role of Jesus in relationship to a new exodus and a new entrance into the
promised land. Some of the complex ways in which these
typological interpretations were put in writing seem
to be reflected in Christian gospels. The next chapter
will show how this might have taken place.

ENDNOTES

1. _HE_ 10.iv.3, 6, 45.
2. _HE_ 10,iv.36.
3. _HE_ 10.iv.3, 6.
4. D. Daube, _The Exodus Pattern in the Bible_ (London, 1963).
5. Lev 25:42; Deut 5:14-15.
6. C. Carmichael, _Law and Narrative in the Bible_ (Ithaca, 1985), pp. 82-83.
7. C. Carmichael, "A New View of the Origin of the Deuteronomic Credo," _VT_ 16 (1969):273-89.
8. Deut 26:1-11.
9. Gen 33.
10. Deut 1; Num 13.
11. Num 20
12. G. W. H. Lampe and K. J. Woollcombe, _Essays on Typology_ (London: SCM Press, c1957), pp. 60-61.
13. Ibid., pp. 34-37.
14. 1 Kgs 17:1-2; 2 Kgs 2:15.
15. Mal 2:7.
16. Mal 3:2-3.
17. Mal 4:5.
18. Matt 21.
19. John 1:21.
20. Lampe and Woollcombe, _Essays_, pp. 42-44.
21. Dan 2:1
22. Gen 41:1.
23. Dan 2:1, 3.
24. Gen 41:8.
25. Dan 2:2.
26. Gen 41:8.
27. Dan 2:3-7.
28. Gen 41:8.
29. Dan 2:14-25.
30. Gen 41:9-14.
31. Dan 2:27-45.
32. Gen 41:25-32.
33. Dan 2:46-47.
34. Gen 41:37-39.
35. Dan 2:48.
36. Gen 41:39-41.
37. Lampe and Woollcombe, _Essays_, p. 42.
38. Num 25.
39. 1 Macc 2:17-28.
40. See GWB, "The Priestly Teacher of Righteousness," _RQ_ 6 (1969):553-58; "The Office of the Teacher of Righteousness," _RQ_ 9 (1977):415-25; and M. Bergman, "Another Reference to 'A Teacher of Righteousness' in Midrashic Literature," _RQ_ 37 (1979):97-98.

41. John 9:1-41.
42. Acts 3:1-4:22.
43. Acts 14:8-10.
44. Lk 8:49-56.
45. Acts 9:36-43.
46. Mk 5:25-34.
47. Acts 5:15.
48. Acts 19:11-12.
49. Matt 9:1-8; Mk 2:1-12; Lk 5:17-26.
50. Acts 9:32-35.
51. Lk 9:51, 53.
52. Acts 19:21; 20:22; 21:15, 17; 23:11.
53. Lk 23:4, 14, 22.
54. Acts 25:25.
55. On this see GWB, The Consequences of the Covenant (Leiden, 1970), pp. 9-18.
56. Deut 15:12-13, 18; Lev 25:8-10.
57. Deut 28:20-21, 41, 64.
58. Deut 29:3-10.
59. Josh 2:1-24.
60. Josh 3:7-17.
61. Josh 5:13-15.
62. Josh 23:1-16.
63. Josh 24:1-28.
64. Deut 15:18.
65. Jer 34:17.
66. Jer 16:18.
67. Isa 61:7.
68. Isa 40:2.
69. Isa 40:2
70. Isa 35.
71. Deut 32:8-11.
72. Isa 40:31
73. Exod 14:15; Isa 63:12-14.
74. Isa 43:2; 51:11.
75. Exod 14:19-20.
76. Isa 52:12; 58:8.
77. Exod 15:3.
78. Isa 42:13.
79. Isa 41:12; 54:14-17.
80. See further GWB, Jesus: the King and his Kingdom (Macon, 1984), pp. 264-68.
81. Ant 14.303-304.
82. Ant 14.321.
83. Lev 25:1-17.
84. Heb 3:1-4:13.
85. See further GWB, To the Hebrews (Garden City, 1972), pp. 52-83.
86. For a more extensive defense of cyclical time in the ancient Near East and its relevance to biblical literature, see GWB, Jesus, pp. 253-83.

87.   Barn 7:3
88.   Barn 7:6-11.
89.   Barn 8:1-5.
90.   Isa 65:2; Barn 8:2-4.
91.   Barn 8:5-7.
92.   Barn 12:8-11.
93.   G. Von Rad, "Typological Interpretation of the Old Tes-tament," tr. J. Bright, C. Westermann (ed.), Essays on Old Testament Hermeneutics (Richmond, c1963), p. 22.
94.   A. Harnack, Marcion, Das Evangelium vom fremden Gott (Leipzig, 1924), pp. 215-33.
95.   Ibid. pp. 22-23; C. Westermann, "The Interpretation of the Old Testament," Essays, pp. 40-43.
96.   P. Fairbairn, The Typology of Scripture (Grand Rapids, n. d.).
97.   Ibid., p. 37.
98.   R. C. Trench, Notes on the Parables of our Lord (London, 1870), pp. 12-147. Von Rad, Essays, p. 23.
99.   J. S. Semler, Versuch einer freiern theologischen Lehr-art (Halle: C. H. Hemmerle, 1777), p. 86, fn. 96.
100.   Westermann, Ibid., p. 43.
101.   Ibid., p. 43.
102.   Ibid., pp. 43-46.
103.   J. Danielou, From Shadow to Reality, tr. W. Hibberd (London, c1960); W. Eichrodt, Theology of the Old Testament, 2 vols., tr. J. A. Baker (Philadelphia, 1967); W. Vischer, The Witness of the Old Testament to Christ, tr. A. B. Crabtree (London, c1949), vol. 1; and G. Von Rad, Old Testament Theo-logy, 2 vols, tr. D. M. G. Stalker (New York, 1962). L. Gop-pelt, Typos: the Typological Interpretation of the Old Testa-ment in the New, tr. D. H. Madvig, foreword, E. E. Ellis (Grand Rapids, 1982).
104.   Danielou, Shadows, pp. 11-13.
105.   Ibid., pp. 44-45.
106.   Ibid., p. 192; P.G. LI 248.
107.   Ibid., p. 157.
108.   W. Vischer, Witness, pp. 12-25.
109.   Ibid., p. 27.
110.   Ibid., p. 114.
111.   Rom 5:12-20. W. Eichrodt, "Is Typological Exegesis an Appropriate Method?", tr. J. Barr, Essays, p. 225.
112.   Ibid., p. 226.
113.   Ibid., p. 229.
114.   Ibid., pp. 234-35.
115.   Ibid., pp. 234-35.
116.   W. A. Irwin, "A Still Small Voice . . . Said, What are You Doing Here?" JBL 78 (1959):9.
117.   Ibid., pp. 5-6.
118.   D. L. Baker, "Typology and the Christian Use of the Old Testament," SJT 29 (1976):149.

119. Baumgaertel, "The Hermeneutical Problem of the Old Testament," Essays, pp. 134-59; Eichrodt, "Typological," Essays, 240-42.
120. H. W. Wolff, "The Hermeneutics of the Old Testament," Essays, p. 174.
121. Goppelt, Typos, p. 198.
122. G. Von Rad, "Typological," p. 17.
123. Isa 11:6-8; Amos 9:1.
124. Amos 9:11.
125. Hos 2:16-20; Isa 52:11-12.
126. Goppelt, Typos, pp. 18-19; Isa 1:21-26.
127. Ibid., p. 28.
128. Ibid., pp. 36-38.
129. Ibid., p. 198.
130. Ibid., p. 199.
131. Ibid., p. 199.
132. Ibid., p. 200.
133. Ibid., p. 201.
134. Ibid., p. 202.
135. Ibid., pp. 225-26.
136. Baker, "Typology," pp. 149-50.
137. Ibid., pp. 150-52.
138. Ibid., pp. 152-54.
139. For an almost exhaustive analysis of works on typology, see R. M. Davidson, Typology in Scripture (Berrien Springs, Mich., c1981). For good bibliographies on typology see both Davidson, Typology, and Baker, "Typology."
140. Davidson, Typology.
141. Ibid., p. 141.
142. See also LXX Exod 25:40.
143. Also in 3 Macc 3:30.
144. Rom 6:17.
145. Davidson, Typology, pp. 147-152.
146. Phil 3:17.
147. Davidson, Typology, pp. 153-57.
148. Ibid., pp. 157-61.
149. Ibid., pp. 164-69; 1 Tim 1:16; 2 Tim 1:13.
150. Ibid., pp. 177-81.
151. Ibid., pp. 203-15.
152. Num 21:17-18.
153. Pseudo-Philo, Biblical Antiquities 10:7.
154. Davidson, Typology, pp. 193-270. This last quote is from p. 270, with an English translation given here for the Greek in Davidson's text.
155. Ibid., pp. 294-96. For a scriptural example of far-fetched typology, based on trivial details, see the exegesis of Melchizedek (Heb 7).
156. Davidson, Typology, pp. 267-68.
157. BJ 6.268-69.
158. GWB, Jesus, p. 253, fn.1.
159. Eccles 1:6, 9.

160.   1QS 10:1-9.
161.   SO 3:289, 627.
162.   Assump Mos 12:4.
163.   2 Bar 53:12; 56:1-69; 4 Ezra 14:11-12.
164.   Rev 9:15.
165.   Deut 18:18.
166.   Isa 35:11.
167.   Isa 35:6.
168.   Isa 35:7; 41:17-18; 43:19-20; 44:3-4.
169.   Isa 35:3-10; 40:10-11; 42:16-20; 50:3.
170.   Isa 43:2; 51:11.
171.   R. Bultmann, "Ursprung und Sinn der Typologie as hermeneutische Methode," TLZ 75 (1950):205-12. One of the scholars
who seems to have recognized the inherent relationship between
typology and cycles is Prof. M. D. Goulder. See his excellent
analysis of the Acts of the Apostles, Type and History (London,
1964).

CHAPTER TWO

MYSTERIES OF MATTHEW

VIEWS OF OTHERS

Bacon. Bacon observed that there were five summary
statements in Matthew that were employed as transition
sentences from one major topic to another.[1] Each of
these transition sentences begins, "Now it happened
when Jesus had finished..." From Matt 3:1-26:1, Bacon
claimed there was a well-structured book composed of
five orderly divisions. Matt 1:1-2:23, then, he considered to be a preamble and 26:2-28:20, the epilogue.
The five division document in between the preamble and
the epilogue, Bacon thought, was patterned in a structure that imitated the Pentateuch's five books. This
was an important observation that has been accepted by
many succeeding scholars,[2] although many others have
taken issue with Bacon on parts of his theory. The
part of his conjecture that has mustered the most support is Bacon's outline based around the transition
sentences.[3] Kingsbury, however, thought even these
were only conclusions to the five major speeches and
not part of a planned "Pentateuch."[4]

Farrer. Among those who were dissatisfied with Bacon's
solution was Farrer,[5] because it placed the birth narratives as well as the death and resurrection accounts
outside the framework of the gospel. Another reason
why Farrer objected to the Pentateuchal approach is
that the five books thus outlined do not follow the
Pentateuch in order, with the first book as an imitation of the Book of Genesis and the second division as
an Exodus. These difficulties led Farrer to suggest a
hexateuchal pattern, including the five books of Moses
and Joshua. The addition of Joshua to the five seemed
natural for Christians whose leader was the new Joshua.[6] Farrer then classified the birth narratives as a
"Genesis,"[7] and considered "Exodus" to begin with Herod's slaughtering of the male children.[8] Leviticus,
Numbers, and Deuteronomy Farrer thought to be less
neatly organized and not really complete documents.

In his first work on this topic, Farrer said
these books consist of discourses that "stripe" Matthew in the proper order, but do not have sharp beginnings and endings. Leviticus consists of chapter 10,
the commissioning of the disciples; Numbers is chapter

13; and Deuteronomy consists of chapter 18, leaving material between the books with no parallel.[9] Joshua began with Jesus' passage through Jericho.[10] "Any real demarcation between Exodus, Leviticus, and Numbers narratives is as difficult to find in St. Matthew as it is in the Pentateuch; the divisions between the middle three Mosaic books are purely artificial," according to Farrer.[11]

Assuming that Matthew used Mark, Farrer concluded that Mark did not form a Hexateuch but that it began and ended hexateuchally so that it "could easily suggest itself to St. Matthew."[12] Matthew "would scarcely find in his predecessor the hint for an expression of the hexateuchal typology by means of set pieces standing out from their contexts. Suggestions for set pieces for formal discourses can be found in St. Mark, but there is nothing specially hexateuchal about them."[13] Farrer devoted only a few pages to this subject and he did not claim much satisfaction for his efforts. It may not have quite so many difficulties as the Pentateuchal theory, but it had more than enough problems to keep Farrer from finding "comfort in a hypothesis."[14] He wished not to "claim any higher status for it than that of likely guesswork."[15]

It is very unlikely that any other scholar can find the comfort in this hypothesis that any Western scholar would like, because Jews and Christians of New Testament times were more easily satisfied than we are about some things. It takes more to persuade the objective analyst than it does to convince a dogmatist of a position in which he already believes. These early scholars searched the HS, their current situation, and available materials in their efforts to prove their preconceived opinions. They were convinced that everything that was in the world was in the Torah, that all prophecy was to be fulfilled in the days of the Messiah, and that these were the days of the Messiah.

Rabbis were amazingly skillful in forcing a situation to prove that some prophecy had been fulfilled, some typology had found a new antitype in the current situation, or some desired situation had been proved by a text. For example, R. Nathan said God showed Abraham the four kingdoms that would oppress his children in the future. This is proved by the text, "Now it happened, as the sun was going down, a deep sleep fell upon Abram, and look, a dread, great darkness, was falling upon him.[16] A dread--this is Ba-

41

bylon; darkness--this is Media; great is the Greek kingdom; was falling is the fourth kingdom, wicked Rome."[17] There is nothing in the text itself to suggest this identification, but the fact that a rabbi could imagine it seemed to "prove" the case. Since they were convinced in advance, inadequate data supported by strained logic was sufficient for them to overlook contradicting data and accept imagined conclusions as "proof." Western scholars will probably continue to be dissatisfied with the kind of guesswork that is required to follow the logic that went into the formation of New Testament and other rabbinic literature.

Vischer had earlier tried to find typological relationships between the HS and the NT. He went through the entire HS, discussing the content of each book. Where he could he found parallels in the NT. In his Genesis chapter, he said, "In harmony with this, according to the narrative of Matthew's gospel, the 'Son of Abraham' who fulfills all things shall in his 'Genesis'[18] and tenderest childhood recapitulate the early history of Israel and fulfill the word of the prophet: 'Out of Egypt have I called my son.'"[19] He found other passages in the Genesis chapter that corresponded to Matthew. He also found parallels in his Exodus chapter to John 6 and 1:14,[20] and in his Leviticus chapter he found comparisons with Mark and Luke,[21] but he did not call these as Mark, Luke, or John's "Exodus," or "Leviticus" sections. In his Joshua chapter, Vischer said that Joshua was very close to the Pentateuch, following immediately after the law, just as Acts followed right after the new contract, and Vischer tried to find parallels between Joshua and Acts. He compared, for instance, Joshua's intent to take the entire land of Palestine to the commission in Acts 1:1-12 to be witnesses to the entire earth.[22] All of this was thought-provoking and may have initially inspired Farrer to develop this line of thinking more coherently.

Evans compared the travel narrative in Luke with the Book of Deuteronomy to show their striking resemblance both in subject matter and organization.[23] This was sufficiently convincing for him to conjecture that the travel narrative was consciously structured after the typology of the Book of Deuteronomy. That which Evans did with one section of Luke will be attempted here with all three synoptic gospels to learn the extent to which these gospels fit into a hexateuchal form such as Farrer suggested but did not pursue

to his own satisfaction. Farrer's belief that a hexateuchal pattern for a document should follow in the
same order as the HS Hexateuch is well taken. His observation that the boundaries between pentateuchal
books themselves is not clear is also valid. There is
much duplication, overlapping, and repetition in the
Pentateuch itself. A typologist, following these books
as a pattern would have had a good deal of freedom,
however, because he would not have had to show a one-
to-one imitation, but only a general outline. This
would have enabled him to pick some items and omit
others and still follow his type to some degree. The
more points the gospel writer followed and the fewer
omissions he made the easier it would be to follow his
outline. This situation also makes twentieth century
scholars' attempts at following this logic guesswork.
It is easy for current scholars also to force parallels and types that were not originally intended.

This kind of guesswork walks across all sorts
of mine fields as if they were peaceful meadows and
leaves many unanswered questions and uncertainties.
Nonetheless, the HS itself contains many typologies
and literary forms patterned after earlier forms and
messages. It is certain that NT authors were not free
from typological deductions, even if we are unable to
find where they all are.[24] This prompts us to undertake the kind of analysis that is doomed in advance to
be more suggestive than convincing. Readers are not
likely to agree on the value of this work, but some
may pursue individual sections more thoroughly than
has been done here to provide more insight into the
nature of the literary form, "Gospel."

When Second Isaiah envisioned the release of
the captives from Babylon and the return and restoration of the promised land, he had the exodus from
Egypt and the conquest of Canaan with their related
events as a pattern or type by which to expect the
deliverance and establishment of the kingdom in his
day. In NT times, the expectation of deliverance from
the Romans and restoration of the kingdom was strong.
This time, however, Jews had the experience of two deliverances and two exoduses in their past history upon
which to base their hopes. For instance, there was a
promise of healing,[25] and Miriam was healed of her
leprosy.[26] Likewise Second Isaiah promised that those
in Babylon with infirmities would be healed.[27] Furthermore, the suffering of the servant in Second Isaiah was given more prominence than Moses's suffering
for the Israelites as the Lord's servant in the Penta-

43

teuch. First century Jews, then, expected healing miracles before the land would be restored; they probably also expected a suffering servant.[28] Gospel writers, even if they patterned their documents basically after the Hexateuch in association with the exodus from Egypt had also to make prominent such things as healing miracles and vicarious suffering which were not as central in the Hexateuch.

Danielou observed that Jewish writers gave very little typological attention to Joshua. Even the writings of Philo give Joshua no place. The most outstanding passage was in Ben Sira 46:1, and he was given slight mention in 4 Ezra 7:107. Goodenough's explanation for this phenomenon is as follows: "The journey which Philo describes never reached the Promised Land. He would undoubtedly have been obliged to explain why Moses could not bring the people into it, and why Joshua must appear greater than him. Thus this could not be discussed."[29] That is only one possibility. Some others are: 1) Philo only intended to write commentaries on the books of the Torah, which were the word of God without any question; 2) Philo may at one time have written about Joshua, but later Jewish editors destroyed them after they learned how important Joshua was to Christian polemics; 3) Later Jews would have avoided giving attention to Joshua for the same reason.

For the church fathers, Joshua was very important--much more important than Moses. It was Joshua who led the army while Moses stood on the mountain and held up his hands. Joshua succeeded in leading the people into the promised land after Moses had failed. Joshua performed the effective circumcision and renewed the contract. Joshua was the type for which Jesus was the antitype. The old Joshua appointed the twelve who were to divide the inheritance, just as Jesus appointed the apostles to announce the truth to the whole world; he began his government at the Jordan, just as Christ, after baptism in the Jordan, began his gospel.[30] Origen said with the death of Moses came the destruction of the law.[31] This probably explains why Farrer was able to discover typological parts of a Hexateuch in Matthew, rather than just a Pentateuch as Bacon attempted. The Hexateuch took Joshua, the type of Jesus, into account.

Because Bacon and Farrer both gave primary

attention to Matthew when comparing a gospel with the
first books of the OT, Matthew will be given the first
examination here without prejudging the order in which
the synoptic gospels were written.

THE GOSPEL OF MATTHEW

Genesis

Gen 5:1: "This is the Book of the Genesis of men . . . "	Matt 1:1: "The Book of the Genesis of Jesus Christ..."
(Hautê hê biblos geneseôs anthropôn	(Biblos geneseôs Iêsou Christou).

The quotation taken from the Septuagint was
probably used as a representative quotation, func-
tioning as an antitype to the whole etiological section, on the one hand, and as an introduction to the
Book of Genesis on the other. The etiological stories
provide a background for the history of the Hebrew
people beginning with Abraham.[32]

Gen 12:1-36:43: Stories of the patriarchs, beginning with Abraham, and lists of their posterity, prior to the activity of Joseph.	Matt 1:2-17: Listing of the patriarchs, beginning with Abraham as ancestors of Jesus, prior to the time of Joseph.
Gen 37:1-50:26: Stories of Joseph, including his dreams and chastity in relationship to to Potiphar's wife. Also his migration to Egypt to save the sons of Israel.	Matt 1:18-2:15: Joseph's dreams and chastity and virtue in relationship to Mary. His flight to Egypt to save the Son.

It would have been still a happier arrangement
if the author could have included the birth of Jesus
in his Exodus section, as Moses's birth was reported
in Exodus.[33] Another similarity between the Moses story and Matthew's story of Jesus is that neither account describes a boyhood. Both jump from birth to
adulthood.

Exodus

Exod 1:1-2:25: Change of kings; slaughter of male children by the king; Moses's	Matt 2:16-23: Slaughter of male children by the king;

45

flight from Egypt.

change of kings; journey of Jesus from Egypt to Nazareth.

Exod 4:27-31: Aaron addressed the Israelites; the people

believed and rejoiced that God had visited his people. They believed and worshipped.

Matt 3:1-2: John addressed the Israelites. All Jerusalem, Judea, and all the region around the Jordan came to him, confessing their sins and being baptized.

Exod 14:1-15:21: Children of Israel approach the Red Sea

and come through it.

Matt 3:13-17: Jesus approaches the Jordan River and is baptized.

Exod 15:22-17:16: Moses and the Israelites were taken up from the sea and went into the wilderness.

After three days, the people

complained that they were thirsty. Moses performed a

miracle to change the bitter water to sweet water. "There

he tempted him" (15:25). When the Israelites were hungry the

Lord tempted them to see if they would obey his law, by

giving them enough manna for each day, but none to pre- serve except for the Sabbath. When Israelites were again

thirsty, Moses criticized them for tempting the Lord (17:2), but he gave in to avoid being stoned (17:4), and performed a miracle to provide water. They called the place "Tempta- tion," because of tempting the

Matt 4:1-11: Jesus was led up from the River Jordan into the wil- derness by the Spirit to be tempted by the devil. After forty days and forty nights of fasting,[34] Jesus was hungry. Then the tempter urged him to perform miracles to provide food, but he refused in obedience to the law (Deut 8:3). Also in obedience to the law he refused to perform a miracle to prevent having a stone strike his foot (4:6), while astonishing the peo- ple at the temple. Unlike the Israel- ites in the wilder- ness, he did not tempt the Lord (Deut 6:16; Matt 4:7).

Lord by saying they wondered if the Lord was with them or not.

Moses commanded Joshua (tô Iêsou) (17:9) to go out to fight Amalek, while Moses promised to stand on top of

a high hill and hold a rod

over the battlefield as Israel conquered Amalek, so that Joshua could win.

The devil took Jesus (Iêsous) up to a very high mountain (4:8) and promised him the kingdoms of the world if he would worship the devil. Jesus again obeyed the law (Deut 5:9; 6:13) in refusing the the temptation.

Exod 19:1: After three

months in the wilderness,

the Israelites came to Mount Sinai.

Matt 4:12-5:1: After John was imprisoned, Jesus journeyed around the tribes of Israel, and then went up to the mountain.

Exod 20:1-17: Commandments

given from Mount Sinai.[35]

Matt 5:2-12: Beatitudes given from the mountain.

Exod 20:18-23:33: More detailed rules to follow in

keeping the commandments.

Matt 5:13-48: More exacting rules to follow than the commandments.

Exod 24:1-40:38: Directions

for worship and sacrifice, details for preparing a tent of meeting, consecration of priests, atonement for sins, free will offerings received with public announcements.

Matt 6:1-7:27: Directions for giving without public announcement, praying, fasting, and forgiveness of sins. An attitude of trust and rigorous ethic demanded.

Matt 7:28: "And it happened when Jesus finished these words, the crowds were astonished at his teaching, 29) for he was teaching them as one who had authority, and not as their scribes."

Matt 2:16-7:29 is a well structured "Exodus," beginning with the slaughter of the male children by the king and following through the proper sequence events similar to those recorded in the Book of Exodus until they had been given the commandments, more explicit rules of behavior, and worship necessary for entrance into the promised land. In Matthew, also, the section ends around the mountain with the crowds receiving further rules necessary for entrance into the kingdom. Furthermore this section, which ends the "Exodus" section of Matthew also concludes with the transition formula noticed by Bacon. The theory that the book's division is at this point is further confirmed by the content of the material in the verses immediately following, which are related to the Book of Leviticus and also Second Isaiah.

Leviticus

It is evident that the author intended to move from Exodus to Leviticus after his transition sentence,[36] because the very next chapter began with Jesus confronting a leper who needed cleansing. Jesus <u>touched</u> him--a practice Leviticus would not have approved--but then told him to fulfill the requirements of the law given in Leviticus.[37] But the ruling of leprosy is not treated in Leviticus until the thirteenth and fourteenth chapters, and the material in Matthew, though well organized, does not parallel Leviticus in order the way the previous sections did. Matthew apparently was not a devoted exponent of Leviticus, because Jesus was shown touching and being touched by unclean people. But Second Isaiah promised that the lame would leap like a ram, the dumb would sing,[38] and the eyes of the blind would be opened.[39]

Therefore the Messiah should be shown fulfilling these expectations. Since traditionally the priests and Levites cleanse the unclean, healing miracles, most of which involved driving out unclean spirits, might properly replace the Levitical rules of the priests.[40] This Matthew did. He introduced the section on miracles with a leper cleansing that referred the cleansed man to the rules of Leviticus. He notified the reader that he was relating Second Isaiah to the Levitical section by a general summary that Jesus had cast out many spirits of those who possessed demons to fulfill the prophecy, "Therefore he has borne our sicknesses and carried our pain."[41] Furthermore, the author confined his healing miracles to the Levitical section and chose exactly ten miracles: 1) cleansing the leper;[42] 2) healing the paralytic;[43] 3) healing the woman of fever;[44] 4) stilling the storm;[45] 5) healing Gedarine demoniacs;[46] 6) forgiving sins of a paralytic so that he could walk;[47] 7) healing the woman of a hemorrhage of twelve years;[48] 8) raising the daughter of a ruler;[49] 9) restoring the sight of two blind men;[50] and 10) casting out a demon of a dumb man so that he could speak.[51]

The ten miracles Jesus performed in Matt 8-9 were probably intended to remind readers of the ten plagues which Aaron sent upon the Egyptians just before Moses led the Israelites out of captivity.[52] The miracles of Egypt were reported in Exodus rather than Leviticus, and they were harming, rather than healing, miracles, but they were performed by Aaron the Levite.[53] Then, in keeping with the imagery of Second Isaiah, Jesus saw the crowd as sheep without a shepherd.[54] Chapter ten began in proper sequence with Jesus commissioning the disciples to heal the sick, raise the dead, cleanse the lepers, and cast out the demons,[55] just as Jesus had been shown doing in Matt 8-9. Matt 8-10, then, included the healing ministry of Jesus and the commissioning of the disciples to continue the same ministry. Jesus' commissioning of the disciples was like Moses' consecration of the priests and assignment of their duties--also reported in Leviticus.[56] The whole section concludes with Jesus' claim that he would cause division among family members,[57] just as Levi had earlier rejected his family to keep the contract.[58]

Matt 8-10 forms a well structured literary section, apart from any attempt to understand its relationship to the Pentateuch. It is seen to represent Leviticus by its beginning with a leper cleansing and concluding with Jesus acting in accordance with the Levites. In between were miracles such as Second Isaiah promised, classed together with one leper cleansing. The ten miracles may have alluded to the ten plagues performed in Egypt by a Levite, and the commissioning of the disciples resembled Moses's commissioning the priests. The author alluded to Leviticus, while at the same time, displacing it with healing miracles that included touching the unclean and showing Jesus to be superior to the Levites. The Leviticus section began after the summary statement following the conclusion of the Exodus section, and was concluded by the following transition sentence, noticed by Bacon.

Matt 11:1: "And it happened when Jesus finished lining up the twelve disciples, he left there so as to teach and preach in their cities."

Num 1:47-4:49: Importance of the Levites who were not to be numbered. In charge of the tabernacle. Nadab and

Abihu killed because they

offered unholy fire (3:4).

Assigned specific tasks. Levites belong to the Lord.

Matt 11:2-15: Jesus' answer to the priest, John, a partial quotation from Isaiah to which was added the promise of good news for the poor (Isa 61:1). Lists the acts Jesus and his disciples did according to Matt 8-10--superior to the Levites. It was a summary, relating the "Numbers" section to the "Leviticus" section in Matthew as they are in the Pentateuch. Matthew's attitude toward Leviticus is the same here as in Matt 8-10. John was identified with Elijah, the messenger who was promised to purify the corrupt Levites.[59]

Num 11:1-30: The Israelites grumbled. Nothing could satisfy them.

Matt 11:16-19: Neither John nor Jesus could could satisfy the people, even though they used different methods.

Num 33-35: The Lord in anger afflicted Israel with plagues.

Matt 11:20-24: Jesus criticized some cities in Israel and promised them destruction on the day of judgment.

Num 12:3: Moses considered the meekest man on earth.

Matt 11:29: "For I am meek and lowly of heart, and you will find rest for your souls."

Num 15:32-36: Man caught pick-

Matt 12:1-12: Jesus'

ing up sticks on the Sabbath.

Put in custody until they could decide what to do with him. Finally stoned him to death.

disciples picked grain on the Sabbath. Accused by the Pharisees. Jesus healed on the Sabbath. Concluded it was lawful to do good on the Sabbath. Opposite conclusions given by Moses and Aaron.

Num 16:1-17:3: The religious (Levites) led a rebellion

against Moses and Aaron. They were punished.

Matt 12:22-45: Religious leaders (scribes and Pharisees) led an attack against Jesus. Jesus gave a rebuttal.

Num 23-24: Balaam blessed and described a glowing future for Israel.

Matt 13:1-52: Jesus told a parable about the future Kingdom of God, its greatness and its coming.

Matt 13:53: "And it happened when Jesus finished these parables, he went away from there."

The division in Matthew that corresponds to Numbers in the Pentateuch is the same division that Bacon noted as a separate unit.[60] Like the "Leviticus" section, it had two divisions, the first comprised two chapters and the second consisted of one. Further agreement in organization is that like chapters 8 and 9, chapters 11 and 12 described activity of Jesus, whereas chapters 10 and 13 were teaching sections or discourses of Jesus. Just as Numbers began with an extensive treatise on the Levites, so the "Numbers" section of Matthew devoted attention at the beginning to the Levites whom John came to cleanse and whose ministry was succeeded by the superior ministry. The rebellious Levites of Numbers were replaced in Matthew by the rebellious scribes and Pharisees. The blessed land and people prophesied in Numbers was countered by the parables about the Kingdom of God. The "Numbers" section is coherent with the "Leviticus" section; it begins after the familiar transition passage and continues until at the end of the section, there is another similar transitional sentence. "Numbers" differed from "Leviticus" in that it followed Numbers in proper sequence.

Deuteronomy

Deut 1:19-46: Moses told the Israelites to enter the land promised them.

People doubted Moses's wisdom and sent spies. They brought back a bad report. Later they failed to enter the land, because they doubted the Lord.

Matt 13:54-58: Jesus entered his own fatherland. He taught the people, but they doubted the wisdom of his teaching. They were scandalized because of him. He could not do mighty deeds there because of their lack of faith.

Deut 1:41-2:1: After defeat by the Amorites, Moses led the Israelites to the wilderness.

Matt 14:1-14: After the death of John the people followed Jesus to the wilderness.

Deut 2:26-35: Could not buy food from Sihon, so conquered the land and took cattle and

booty.

Matt 14:15-21: People could not buy food in the wilderness. Jesus multiplied the loaves and fishes so that there was more than enough.

Deut 3:1-29: The Lord showed the people his greatness by conquering nations for them.

Moses asked to see more but was not allowed because of the sin of Moses and the people earlier.

Matt 14:22-36: Jesus performed many great deeds, stilling the storm, walking on the water and healing diseases. Peter asked to be able to walk on water, but he could not, because he lacked faith.

Deut 4:44-6:25: Commandments and admonitions to keep them. Rewards and punishments for keeping and breaking commandments. Moses foresaw that Israelites would break commandments and be scattered.

Matt 15:1-14: Conflict with Pharisees over the commandments. Pharisees had broken them and would be uprooted.

Deut 7:12-16: Those who keep commandments will be prosperous and all sickness will be healed by the Lord.

Matt 15:21-31: Jesus healed demon possessed, dumb, blind, maimed, and lame, so

that the multitudes
glorified the God of
Israel.

Deut 8:1-10: Lord let Israelites be hungry and fed them
manna that they might know
that man does not live by
bread alone.

Matt 15:32-39: Jesus
fed the hungry multi-
tude multiplying the
loaves and fishes.

Deut 9:1-6: Children of Israel
to cross the Jordan "this day"
and receive

the promised land.

Matt 16:24-28: Jesus
promised that some who
were standing there
would not die before
they saw the Son of
man coming into his
kingdom.

Deut 9:9-29: Moses went up to
the mountain to receive
the commandments.
He
returned to find Israelites
worshipping the golden calf.

Moses broke the tablets in
anger.

Prayer for Aaron and the
people.

Matt 17:1-20: Jesus
went up to the moun-
tain with Peter,
James, and John. He
returned to find dis-
ciples unable to heal
a boy possessed of
demons. Jesus was an-
gry because the disci-
ples lacked faith.
Said prayer could
move mountains.

Deut 14:1-28: "You are the
sons of the Lord your God."
Rules for giving tithes for
the temple and for Levites
and others who did not have
land.

Matt 17:24-26: Sons
are free. Aliens are
to pay taxes.

Deut 17:1-13: Procedure for
dealing with a man who had

broken contract. At the evidence of two or three witnesses, he should be put to

death. Provision made for
judges and priests to see

that justice was rendered.

Matt 18:15-20:
Procedure for dealing
with a man who had
sinned within the com-
munity. If he did not
listen, the sin was to
be confirmed by two or
three witnesses. If he
refused to listen
even to the church
he was to be
excommunicated.
"Wherever two or three

are gathered in my
name, there am I in
the midst of them."

Deut 18:9-19:21: Justice
should be rendered fairly and

the offender punished to purge

the evil from the community.
Eye should show no pity.

Matt 18:21-35:
Forgiveness required
of a brother offended
If he does not forgive
he is to be given
strict justice without
mercy.

Matt 19:1: "Now it happened when Jesus had finished these sayings, he went away from Galilee...."

The transition sentence in 19:1 should indicate
the end of one section and the beginning of another,
but it does not. There are several more chapters in
the Book of Deuteronomy, which might be dismissed if
that were the only problem. Since it is not possible
to provide a parallel to everything in the Pentateuch,
the editor or author of Matthew might have followed
the outline up to a certain point and then moved on
into another book, such as Joshua. But the section
from Matt 19:2 ff. does not parallel the first part of
the book of Joshua as might be expected from the previous pattern. Neither does this section properly fit
under a new category. Because of the summary statement
in Matt 19:1, Bacon decided that this was the end of
Jesus' discourse on church administration,[61] so he began with Matt 19:1b to organize a new subject heading
which he called "Division A. Jesus in Judaea. Chh. 19-
22."[62] The material from Matt 19:1b-20:15, however, is
really very similar in content to that found in Matt
17:22-18:35. The section from Matt 20:17-22:46 consists of a unified division which includes further
things Jesus did before he began the great discourse
in Matt 23:1 ff. The discussion of Jesus' moving into
a different geographical area in 19:1 was continued in
20:17. Furthermore, Matt 19:20-20:16 continues in
proper sequence to resemble the continued parallel material in the Book of Deuteronomy, as is indicated be-
low:

Deut 21:15-17: 22:13-30;
24:1-5: Rules of conduct between husbands and wives, including the question of
divorce.

Matt 19:3-12:
Questions concerning
marriage, including
the question of
divorce and celibacy.

54

Deut 26:1-30:20: Exhortations and warnings; promises and condemnations for those who enter the contract and either keep the contract or break it. Those who keep it will have life, and those who break it or do not accept the contract will have death. They have the decision to make.	Matt 19:16-30: Decision of man who came to Jesus and wanted eternal life.
Deut 32:10-43: The Lord found Israel in the wilderness. He led him out and overcame his enemies, promising Jacob his allotted heritage.	Matt 20:1-16: Parable of the kingdom. A landlord who found idle people in the market places; took them to his vineyard to work and gave them full wages against the opposition of other workers.

Matt 13:54-20:16 constitutes a division in the Gospel of Matthew that resembles the Book of Deuteronomy both in order and content. The two problems are: 1) the "transition" sentence that was used to indicate the end of the books of Exodus and Leviticus does not come at the end of the division. This may indicate that the verse has been misplaced in copying or that the material following Matt 19:2 has been added later in between the divisions without transferring the transition sentence to conclude the new additions. If this was so, however, the person who made the additions made them in the proper sequence so as to complete the omitted portion of the Book of Deuteronomy. 2) There is one parallel, noticed by Farrer,[63] and Evans[64] which has been omitted in the above list, because it falls out of sequence, but it is, nonetheless, striking:

Deut 18:15-22: Promise that the Lord will raise up a prophet like Moses. The people will hear him.	Matt 17:1-5: At the Mount of Transfiguration, the voice from heaven said, "This is my beloved son in whom I am well pleased. Hear him!"

The belief that the fifth division of the Book of Matthew ends at 20:16 rather than 18:35 is further confirmed by the content of the material beginning with Matt 20:17, which parallels the beginning of the Book of Joshua. The transition sentence[65] says Jesus went from Galilee, along the territory beyond the Jordan, until he came to Judah in the mountain region. There is no further mention of the territory in which he ministered until after Matt 20:17, where he was on his way to Jerusalem--a natural follow-up from 19:1. This further suggests that at one time Matt 19:1 was followed immediately by Matt 20:17, whether the verses in between were added later or not.

Joshua

Josh 1:1-18: Joshua prepared to enter the land; instructed the offi- cers to be ready.	Matt 20:17-28: Jesus prepared to enter Jerusalem; instructed the twelve to be ready. James and John ask to be made chief officers.
Josh 2:1-24: Joshua sent two spies to Jericho to prepare for the invasion.	Matt 20:29-21:7: Jesus sent two messengers from Jericho to prepare for his entrance.
Josh 3:1-4:24: Joshua was exalted in the sight of Israel as the people under his leadership entered the land.	Matt 21:8-27: Israelites shouted, "Hosanna!" as Jesus with his disciples entered Jerusalem.
Josh 8:1-29: Ai captured, destroyed, and left in a heap of ruins.	Matt 24:1-2: Prophesied destruction of Jerusalem so that one stone would not be left on top of another.
Josh 10:11-14: Great stones from heaven fell on enemy; sun stood still for Joshua.	Matt 24:22, 29: Days were to be shortened for the elect; sun darkened and stars to fall from heaven.
Josh 19:49: "When they had finished distributing their several territories	Matt 26:1: "And it happened when Jesus had finished all these words . . ."

The "transition" sentence,[66] thought to conclude divisions within the Gospel of Matthew is locat-
ed here before the end of the gospel and also before
the end of the Book of Joshua. But it shows some parallel to Joshua 19:49. Josh 19:49 might have been the
passage in the Hexateuch that suggested the formula to
the author or editor which he then used four additional times in the gospel. The other possibility is that
a later scribe moved the verse from its original posi-
tion--wherever that was--to its present location so
that its relationship to Joshua 19:49 would be more
evident. The events which follow in both books continue in the same sequence as was true also of the fifth
division in relationship to the Book of Deuteronomy.

Josh 24:1-26: The renewal of the contract.	Matt 26:2-30: The last supper with Jesus' disciples in which he inaugurated the new contract.
Josh 24:29-30: Death of Joshua.	Matt 27:27-50: Death of Jesus.
Josh 24:32: Bones of Joseph buried at Shechem.	Matt 27:57-60: Joseph buried the body of Jesus.

The "Joshua" section of Matthew[67] began with
Jesus in Judaea at Jericho at the very place where
Joshua had earlier entered the promised land. Jesus
had moved from Galilee across the Jordan so that he
could enter the land at the same place Joshua crossed
before. The entrance into Jerusalem was very similar
to Joshua's entrance into Palestine. Jesus celebrated
the Passover just after his arrival into Jerusalem
just as Joshua had earlier celebrated the Passover
just after his arrival into the land. Since the major
objective of Jesus, according to Matthew, was Jerusalem, Jesus' program was not made to correspond in
order to that of Joshua.[68] Instead, Jesus' Passover
celebration[69] was placed in a position to represent
Joshua's renewal of the contract, because it included
Jesus's inauguration of the new contract. The prophesied fall of Jerusalem[70] might be expected to reflect
the fall of Jericho in Joshua,[71] but in sequence it
falls closer to the destruction of Ai,[72] and the fall
of Jericho has no direct counterpart in Matthew.

The "transition" sentence does not come at the
end of the "Joshua" section of Matthew, but it matches

a corresponding quotation in the Book of Joshua. Even such details as the burial of Joseph's bones in a different tomb was reflected by a Joseph in Matthew who placed Jesus's body in a new tomb. Since there was no resurrection in Joshua, Matt 28 extends beyond the limits of the Hexateuch in the HS.

SUMMARY

This examination has not demonstrated a perfect relationship between the contents and order of events in the Gospel of Matthew and the Hexateuch in the HS, but it would have satisfied those who were already convinced that these were the last days of the evil age. They thought they were in the very position where the Hebrews had been just before the conquest, at the place Babylonian Jews had been just before the invasion of Cyrus into Babylon, and just where Palestinian Jews had been after the temple had been defiled by Antiochus Epiphanes. They were looking for signs that would "prove" their beliefs, and these typologies would have pleased them. The divisions between Exodus and Leviticus and Leviticus and Numbers seem less artificial than Farrer thought them to be. Once these divisions are seen more clearly, a hypothesis seems possible that has at least a little more claim for itself than "likely guesswork."[73]

In review, the Matthaean Hexateuch would be divided as follows:

1. Genesis--Matt 1:1-2:15.
2. Exodus--Matt 2:16-7:27 plus transition sentence.
3. Leviticus--Matt 8:1-10:39 plus transition sentence.
4. Numbers---Matt 11:2-13:52 plus transition sentence.
5. Deuteronomy--Matt 13:54-20:16 with transition sentence displaced at 19:1.
6. Joshua--Matt 20:17-27:60 with transition sentence misplaced at 26:1.
   --Resurrection account in Matt 28.

Bacon's organization of the Matthaean Torah is
as follows:
Prologue--Matt 1:1-2:23.
1. Genesis--Matt 3:1-7:27.
2. Exodus--Matt 8:1:-10:39.
3. Leviticus--Matt 11:2-13:52.
4. Numbers--Matt 13:54-18:35.
5. Deuteronomy--19:1b-25:46.
Epilogue--Matt 26:2-28:20.

Farrer's hexateuchal "stripes" in Matthew seem
to be about as follows:

1. Genesis--Matt 1:1-2:15.[74]
2. Exodus--Matt 5:1-7:27.[75]
3. Leviticus--Matt 10:1-39.[76]
4. Numbers--Matt 12:46-13:58.[77]
5. Deuteronomy--Matt 16:21-18:35.[78]
6. Joshua--Matt 20:29-25:46.[79]

ENDNOTES

1.   B. C. Bacon, Studies in Matthew (New York, c1950), p. 47, 145-335. The transition sentences are: Matt 7:28-29; 11:1; 13:53; 19:1; and 26:1.
2.   For a list of commentators that accept Bacon's proposal, see J. D. Kingsbury, Matthew: Structure, Christology, Kingdom (Philadelphia, c1975), p. 3, fn. 13.
3.   Ibid., p. 3.
4.   Ibid., p. 5.
5.   A. Farrer, St. Matthew and St. Mark (Philadelphia, 1954), p. 179; summarized in "On Dispensing with Q," Studies in the Gospels, ed. D. E. Nineham (Oxford, 1955), pp. 75-77. Later references will be from the book. Unfortunately, Farrer devoted only a few pages, both in his book and in his article, to the subject of hexateuch in the gospels. The idea was his, but he did not develop it.
6.   Farrer, St. Matthew, pp. 177-178.
7.   Ibid., p. 182.
8.   Ibid., pp. 182-183; Matt 2:16.
9.   Ibid., 183-184.
10.   Josh 20:29.
11.   Farrer, St. Matthew, p. 183.
12.   Ibid., p. 187.
13.   Ibid.
14.   Ibid., p. 189.
15.   Ibid., p. 197.
16.   Gen 15:12.
17.   Mek, Bahodesh 9:30-36.
18.   Matt 2:13-15.
19.   Matt 2:13-15; Hosea 11:1; Vischer, Witness, p. 127.
20.   Ibid., p. 185.
21.   Ibid., p. 219.
22.   W. Vischer, Das Christuszeugnis des Alten Testaments (Zuerich, 1946) vol 2, p. 44.
23.   C. F. Evans, "The Central Section of Luke's Gospel," Studies in the Gospels (Oxford, 1957), pp. 42-50.
24.   Farrer and Evans were not the first NT scholars to consider the importance of typology. This was studied years before by D. F. Strauss, The Life of Jesus (London and New York, 1895) passim and L. Goppelt, Typos.
25.   Deut 7:15.
26.   Num 12:12-15.
27.   Isa 35:5-6.
28.   The fact that Jesus as the Messiah was quickly understood as a suffering servant alone suggests that this theology was already known, but there are other reasons that support this supposition: 1) Targum Isa 52:13 renders the Masoretic "my servant" by "my servant, the Messiah." 2) Medieval Judaism expected the Messiah would have to suffer before he ruled (PR

161b–162b; GWB, Revelation and Redemption (Dillsboro, sold by Mercer U. Press, 1978) pp. 71–75, 459–60.

29. E. Goodenough, By Light, Light (New Haven, 1935), p. 221.

30. Cyril of Jerusalem 10:11, PG 33.676B.

31. I.3, 828A–B.

32. Gen 12:1

33. Exod 2:1–10.

34. This ties the temptations of Jesus in Matthew both to the temptations in the wilderness and Jesus' hunger with the people's hunger.

35. There are only nine beatitudes, with eight that were formed together as a unit, and a ninth which the editor composed, perhaps to make them match the nine commandments. In the Masoretic text and LXX, the "second" commandment is only an interpretation of the first (Deut 5:7, 8–10), just as other commandments have interpretations. Philo, who had made a point of telling the importance of the number ten in relationship to the ten commandments, was unable to make a distinction between the first and so-called second commandment (De. Dec. xvii.82). Although in the Samaritan Pentateuch (Sam. text Deut 5:18) the tenth commandment is longer than the other nine, and most scholars, like J. Macdonald, The Samaritan Theology (Philadelphia, c1964), p. 284, and M. Gaster, The Samaritans (London, 1925), p. 185 ff., thought the Samaritan text had compressed the first two commandments and added a tenth which commands worship on Mount Gerizim, the reverse logic is worth considering. Deuteronomy has the marks of an originally Northern document. Even the Jewish text includes two references to Gerizim (Deut 11:29; 27:12) and no direct reference to Jerusalem or any city in Judah. Rabbis tried to modify the strongly northern character of Deuteronomy by rendering Lebanon as the temple, the place where the Lord makes white Israel's sins. Scriptural proof for identifying Lebanon with the temple was Jer 22:5–6. See Sifre, Debarim, 66b #6; 71b #8). It is thought-provoking to note that Matthew matched the commandments with only nine beatitudes.

36. Matt 7:23–29.

37. Lev 8:56; 17:14; 13:49; 14:2–32.

38. Isa 35:6, 11–12.

39. Isa 35:5; 42:7.

40. The term, "unclean spirit," however, was not used in Matthew. Mark made that term popular. Luke also used the expression.

41. Isa 53:4; Matt 8:16–17.

42. Matt 8:1–4.

43. Matt 8:5–13.

44. Matt 8:14–15.

45. Matt 8:23–37—the only one in the section that is not a healing miracle.

46. Matt 8:28–34.

47.   Matt 9:1-8.
48.   Matt 9:18-22.
49.   Matt 9:18, 23-26.
50.   Matt 9:27-31.
51.   Matt 9:32-33.
52.   Exod 7:14-11:10.
53.   Exod 7:10-11:9.
54.   Isa 40:11; Matt 9:36.
55.   Matt 10:8.
56.   Lev 8.
57.   Matt 10:34-39.
58.   Deut 33:8-9.
59.   Mal 3:1, 24; Matt 11:4-6.
60.   Bacon, Studies, pp. 288-296.
61.   Bacon, Studies, pp. 304-307.
62.   Bacon, Studies, p. 308.
63.   Farrer, St. Matthew, p. 186.
64.   Evans, "The Central Section," p. 51.
65.   Matt 19:1.
66.   Matt 26:1.
67.   Matt 20:17-27:26.
68.   Josh 5:10-12.
69.   Matt 26:2-30.
70.   Matt 24:1-12.
71.   Farrer, St. Matthew, p. 184, made that identification.
72.   Josh 8:1-29.
73.   Farrer, St. Matthew, p. 197.
74.   Ibid., p. 182.
75.   Ibid., p. 183.
76.   Ibid., pp. 183, 190.
77.   Ibid., p. 184.
78.   Ibid., pp. 184-85.
79.   Ibid., p. 184.

CHAPTER THREE

THE MARKAN MODEL

INTRODUCTION

Bacon and Farrer both assumed the priority of Mark, so neither looked to see if Mark had made any use of Matthew's five-fold or six-fold structure. Farrer searched for clues of a Hexateuch in Mark that might have influenced the composition of Matthew. He observed that the "Genesis" in Mark was very brief, and he noted two sections to be captioned "Exodus."[1] There was a Deuteronomic phase and a "Joshua" conclusion,[2] but Farrer concluded: "It is unnecessary to suppose that he [Mark] saw his Gospel as a continuous Hexateuch, and as we shall presently show, anyone who tries to construe it as such runs into serious difficulties."[3]

Without minimizing the difficulties involved, this research will proceed to look for a Hexateuch in Mark in just the same way it was done in Matthew. Comparisons will not be attempted except to note variants in passing. Mark will not be followed from a Matthew position, but will be examined for its own outline that it either discloses or fails to disclose. The reason for this is plain. If only Matthew shows a Hexateuch, then this form is typically and uniquely Matthaean. If it is found in other gospels, then there may have been a known literary form which they all followed. Since there is some difference in the outlines of the three gospels, it should readily be seen whether or not the Hexateuch shows up only when the gospels agree in outline, showing thereby that one simply reflects the influence of the other, but that the author was unaware of a literary pattern which he followed whether or not he used one or more of the other gospels as sources. To learn which way the pattern was formed the Gospel of Mark will next be examined.

THE GOSPEL OF MARK

Genesis

Gen 1:1: In the beginning (archê) God created heaven and earth . . . "

Mk 1:1: "The beginning (archê) of the gospel of Jesus Christ . . . "

Farrer was correct in concluding that this was a very brief "Genesis," including only three verses (Mk 1:1-3). But Matthew's "Genesis" was only enough larger than Mark's to include Gen 12-50. Mark evidently was interested only in the etiological stories of Gen 1-11 and did not choose to emphasize the importance of the children of Abraham. These three verses were enough for Mark to call attention both to "the beginning" and to the "gospel," the latter by a mention of the word in Mk 1:1 and also by quoting from Isa 40:3. This related the beginning of the Hexateuch with the Book of Isaiah which tells the "gospel" of the restoration of the promised land and also with the events related to Jesus, which were to follow.

Exodus

Mark began his Exodus section by a reference to the wilderness from Second Isaiah (Isa 40:3). This was not surprising. Jews and Christians were convinced that the wilderness report by Second Isaiah was as valid as one from Exodus. Since the wilderness account related to the exodus from Egypt was the type for which the wilderness account in Second Isaiah was the antitype, these were doctrinally the same. Both occurred in the same point in the cycle. The end of the Egypt cycle was the same as the end of the Babylonian cycle and the end of the Seleucid cycle. Paul probably meant something like that when he told the Corinthians that the Hebrew Scripture reports of the wilderness temptations were written as warnings for "us to whom the ends of the ages have coincided."[4] There were more ages and more ends than one involved. At the ends they should all be parallel with all previous ends as types for later ends. The scripture was written so that later believers could search it to find out how things followed in sequence in earlier ages, so that they could predict that which would happen in their own. This is what Mark did. He began his Genesis from the Torah, but he began the "exodus" from Second Isaiah. Mark switched back and forth from one age to the other throughout his Hexateuch. From the Babylonian cycle report of the wilderness, he turned to the allusion to the Egyptian cycle typology of John and Jesus.

Exod 3:1-13:2 : Aaron and Moses.	Mk 1:4-8: John and Jesus.
Exod 14:1-15:27: Crossing the Red Sea.	Mk 1:9-11: Baptism in the Jordan.

Exod 16:1-18:12: Israelites tempt the Lord in the wilderness.

Mk 1:12-13: The Lord tempted by Satan in the wilderness.

Exod 18:13-27: Moses appointed judges to help him.

Mk 1:16-20: Jesus called disciples to help him.

Exod 19:6: Israel is a holy nation (19:16-25). Only Moses could approach God on Mount Sinai.

Mk 1:24: Jesus was the holy one of God.

Mk 1:22: "And they were surprised at his teaching, for he taught them as one who had authority and not as their scribes."

The "Exodus" section in Mark is longer than the "Genesis" section, but it is still smaller than either book in the Gospel of Matthew. The "transition" sentence is only partially quoted here, omitting the characteristic formula, "And it happened when Jesus had finished..." The sentence quoted, however, is quoted in the exact position in the Gospel of Mark as the first "transition" sentence is found in the Gospel of Matthew. Mark and Matthew both concluded the "Exodus" portions of their gospels at this point. Mark also noted the astonishment of Jesus' audiences four more times.

Leviticus

Lev 5:1-13: Rules for becoming cleansed from ritual uncleanness.

Mk 1:23-28: Unclean demon driven from a man.

Mk 1:29-31: Woman cured of a fever.

Lev 13-14: Rules for recognition and cleansing of leprosy.

Mk 1:40-44: Jesus cleansed a leper and told him to fulfill the law given in Lev 13:49.

Isa 35:8: "No unclean thing will pass over it."

Isa 52:11: "Turn away! turn away! Depart from her midst! Purify yourselves, you carriers of the vessels of the Lord."

Lev 6:24-7:10: Rules for obtaining atonement from sin.

Mk 2:1-13: Jesus forgave the paralytic's sins so that he could walk and was healed.

Isa 43:25: "I, I am he who blots out your transgressions for my own benefit, and your sins I will not remember."

Lev. 8:1-36: Moses consecrated Aaron and sons and assigned their duties.

Mk 2:13-14: Jesus called Levi from tax collecting to be his disciple.

Lev 10:4-11:47: Dietary and cleanliness rules for priests (10) and people (11).

Mk 2:15-27: Jesus ate with tax collectors and sinners; disciples did not fast; picked grain on the Sabbath.

Isa 59:2-3: "But your iniquities have made a separation between you and your God, and your sins have hid his face from you so that he does not hear, 3) for your hands are defiled with blood, and your fingers with iniquity; your lips have spoken lies, wickedness."

Mk 3:1-5: A man with a withered hand healed.[5]

Lev 15:1-33: Rules for menstrual and seminal uncleanness.

Mk 3:10-19: Unclean spirits recognize Jesus as the Son of God. Jesus commissioned his twelve and gave them authority to cast out demons.

Isa 64:5: "We have all become like something unclean; all of our righteousness is like a [bride's] testimony garment."

Lev 16:1-34: Day of Atone-

Mk 3:28-29: Discussion

ment for forgiveness of sins and warnings of thing not

to do lest they die.

of sins that can and cannot be forgiven (those whose sins cannot be forgiven are excommunicated or "die.")

Lev 17:1-16: Rules an Israelite must keep or be cut off from his people (note also Deut 33:9, where Levi denied his mother, brothers, and sons).

Mk 3:31-35: Jesus voluntarily cut off from his family to be a member of another group that did the will of God.

Lev 18:1-30: Rules for abstinence from certain relatives.

Lev 19:3 Commandment to honor parents.

Lev 19:9-10: Rules for

harvest. Portions to be left for the poor.

Mk 4:3-20: Parables of the sower and its interpretation. Kinds of harvest.

Lev 19:35-37: Commandment to use just balances, weights, and measures.

Mk 4:24-25: In the measure you measure, it will be measured to you.

Lev 20:1-27: Purity rules that must be kept if Israel-

ites are to stay on the land.

Mk 4:30-33: Acquisition of the Kingdom of God compared to a mustard seed.

Isa 40:12: "Who has measured

the waters in the hollow of his hand and marked off the heavens with a span, enclosed the dust of the earth in a measure and weighed the mountains in scales."

Mk 4:35-41: Stilling the storm.[6]

Isa 44:24: "...I am the Lord, who made all things, who stretched out the heavens alone, who spread out the earth--who was with me?"

67

Isa 45:8: "Shower, O hea-
vens, from above, and let
the skies rain down justice;
let the earth open, that salvation may sprout, and let it
cause righteousness to
spring up also; I, the Lord,
have created it."

Isa 45:12: "I made the earth,
and created man upon it; it
was my hands that stretched
out the heavens, and I commanded their troops."

Isa 50:2: "Look! by my rebuke
I dry up the sea, I make the
rivers a desert."

Isa 51:9-10: "Was it not you
who cut Rahab in pieces,
who stabbed the dragon?
10) Was it not you who dried
up the sea, the waters of
the great deep; that made
the depths of the sea a
way for the redeemed to pass
over?"

Lev 21:1-24: Rules for purity
required of priests. They

must not touch the dead (21:
1, 11).

Isa 64:5: "We have all become

like something unclean; all
our righteousness is like a
[bride's] testimony garment."

Lev 22:1-9: Rules for priests
against uncleanness from
touching corpses or defiled
people.

Isa 65:4: "They live in tombs
and spend the night in secret

Mk 5:1-19: Gerasene
possessed of an un-
clean spirit and liv-
ing among the tombs
healed.

Mk 5:15-34: Woman
healed of a hemor-
rhage.

Mk 5:21-43: Jairus'
daughter touched by
Jesus and raised
from death.

68

places; they eat pork; pieces
of food are in their vessels.
(cf 52:11).

> Mk 6:1-2: "And he went from there and came into
> his fatherland, and his disciples followed him,
> 2) and, since it was on the Sabbath, he began
> to teach in the synagogue, and many, when they
> heard, were surprised."

Just as Mark ended the "Exodus" section of his
gospel with a summary comment, noting the surprise of
Jesus's audience at his teaching, so also his "Leviticus" section ends with a similar summary. The reference to Jesus's home coming, which for Matthew occurred in the "Deuteronomy" section, was here used as
a summary of the "Leviticus" section. Since Mark's material was somewhat differently organized, the commissioning of the disciples, which for Matthew occurred
in the "Leviticus" section, for Mark was twice briefly
reported: once in the early part of his "Leviticus"
section[7] where the names were given, and again in the
"Numbers" section, where more instructions were given.

Since Mark did not include all ten miracles in
the "Leviticus" section, he apparently did not concentrate his reflection of Second Isaiah there as much as
Matthew did. He, instead, quoted from Second Isaiah at
the very beginning of his gospel, and he related this
division of his gospel more closely to Leviticus by
giving more emphasis to the "unclean" nature of the
spirits Jesus cast out than Matthew did. Furthermore,
his "Leviticus" section followed in better sequence of
events than Matthew's did. Mark, who has only sixteen
chapters altogether, devoted four and a half chapters
to the "Leviticus" section, whereas Matthew, with
twenty-seven chapters in his Hexateuch, allowed only
three chapters to the "Leviticus" section.

Numbers

Num 1:44-54; 3:1-4:49: Levites separated, numbered, assigned duties and instructions not to give them land.	Mk 6:7-13: Disciples called apart, assigned duties and given authority, instructed to to take no provisions for their journey.
Num 5:11-31: Rules for deal- ing with an unfaithful wife.	Mk 6:14-29: John the Baptist, killed by Herod, even though he

	was holy and inno- cent, because he cri- ticized Herod for taking his brother's unfaithful wife.
Num 8:1-26: Levites separated from the people of Israel.	Mk 6:3-32: Jesus sepa- rated his disciples from the crowd so that they could be alone together.
Num 9:1-14: Rules for keeping Passover; everyone must do it; none shall be left over; strangers and people on jour- neys must be served.	Mk 6:34-44: Five thou- sand men with Jesus in a desert. Multiplied loaves so that all were served, and bas- kets full of food left over.
Num 11:1-23: People grumbled because they had only manna.	Mk 6:45-52: Jesus walked on the water. Disciples afraid; their hearts were hardened; they did not understand the loaves.
Num 12:1-16: Complaint of Aaron and Miriam against Moses. 14:1-10: People's re- bellion against Moses and Aaron. 16:1-50: Korah's re- bellion against Moses and Aaron.	Mk 7:1-19: Pharisees and scribes criticized the disciples of Je- sus, because they ate with defiled hands. Challenged Jesus's au- thority.
Num 19:1-22: Rules for cleansing uncleanness for Israelite and stranger (19:10).	Mk 7:14-23: Lecture on defilement. Mk 7:24-30: Jesus healed daughter of Sy- rophonician of her unclean spirit (7:15).
Num 22:1-24:25: Balaam's blessing. The Lord opened the mouth of Balaam's ass and it spoke (22:28-30); then he opened the eyes of Balaam (22:31).	Mk 7:32-36: Jesus healed a deaf and dumb so that he could hear and speak.

Mk 7:37: "And they were very much surprised, saying 'He has done everything well; he makes the deaf hear and the dumb speak.'"

The transition sentence in Mark also includes a summary statement about Jesus's skill in healing. The Matthaean parallel to this is Matt 15:31, which belongs to Matthew's "Deuteronomy" section. There is another similar summary in Matt 11:5, which falls into the beginning of Matthew's "Numbers" section. Other parallels with the Book of Numbers in Mark differ from those in Matthew, but they are parallels, nevertheless. This further supports the hypothesis that Mark was intentionally following a known pattern for writing a gospel rather than coincidentally falling into the same outline as Matthew had done. It also argues against Matthew's use of Mark in the same way. Both seemed to use their materials so as to compose sections that resembled the Book of Numbers, even when they were not in agreement between themselves.

Deuteronomy

Deut 2:7: The Lord provided for Israelites in the wilderness for forty years so that they lacked nothing.

Mk 8:1-21: In the wilderness the Lord multiplied loaves so that everyone ate and was satisfied, and there were seven baskets full left over. Discussion of the meaning of the miracle.

Isa 35:6-7: "For waters will break out in the wilderness, and streams, in the desert; the burning sand shall become a pool, and thirsty ground, springs of water."

Isa 41;18-19: "I will open rivers on the bare heights, and fountains in the valleys; I will make the wilderness a pond of water; and the dry land, springs of water, I will put in the wilderness the cedar, the acacia, the myrtle, and the olive; I will set in the desert the cypress, the plane, and the pine

71

together."

Isa 43:20: "For I put water
in the wilderness, rivers in
the desert, to provide drink
for my chosen people."

Isa 48:21: "They were not
thirsty when he led them
through the deserts; he
made water flow from the
rock for them; he split the
rock, and water poured out"

Isa 35:5: "Then shall the   Mk 8:22:27: Jesus
eyes of the blind be opened."   healed a blind man.

Isa 42:7: "To open the blind
eyes."

42:16: "I will lead the blind
in a way they do not know."

42:18: "Pay attention, you
deaf, and look, you blind,
so as to see!"

42:19: "Who is blind except
my servant...? Who is blind
like the one under contract?
blind like the servant of
the Lord?

Deut 2:8-3:17: Moses and   Mk 8:22-27: Jesus and
the Israelites left Seir,   his disciples left
went around Elath and north   Dalmanutha and went to
through Moab, Ammon, and as   Bethsaida, then north
far as Bashan, taking all   to Caesarea Philippi.
the territory north of Moab.

Deut 3:23-29: The Lord told   Mk 8:27-33: The Lord
Moses that Moses must die be-   told the disciples
fore entering the promised   that the Son of man
land.   must suffer and be
Moses charged Joshua.   killed. Jesus rebuked
                                    Peter.

Deut 5:1-33: Moses read the   Mk 9:2-9: Jesus,
ten commandments that the   James, John, and Peter
Lord gave to the assembly   on a high mountain.
out of the midst of the fire,   Jesus was transfigured

the cloud, and deep darkness
at the mountain. They saw
the glory of God and lived,
but were afraid.
People went back,
and Moses
was left alone with God.

before them. Cloud
overshadowed them.
Voice from cloud
quoted Deut 18:15.
Moses and Elijah van-
ished, and Jesus
was left alone before
them.

Deut 9:6-29: Moses came down
from the mountain to find the
people had been unfaithful;

Mk 9:14-29: Jesus came
down from the mountain
to find that the dis-
ciples were not able
to cast out a demon.
Jesus was angry with
them. Asking first if
the father believed,
Jesus cast out the
demon. Jesus told the
disciples that this
could be done only
through prayer.

Moses broke tables in anger.
Then he fasted another forty
days and nights, praying for
those faithless people. Re-
covered the commandments.

Deut 11:18-20: Admonition to
teach these laws to their
children.

Mk 9:33-37: Whoever
receives one child
such as this in
Christ's name . . .

Deut 11:21-32: Promised blessings and curses.

Mk 9:38-50: Promised
rewards and punish-
ments.

Deut 24:1-5: Rules for
divorce raised. Alluded to by
Isa 50:1: "Thus says the Lord:
'Where is your mother's bill
of divorce, with which I put
her away?'"

Mk 10:1-12: Question
of divorce, quoting
Deut 24:1.

Deut 30:1-5: After promised
blessings and curses, if
Israelites and children return to the Lord, then the
Lord will return them from
the scattered nations and
give them the promised land.

Mk 10:13-16: Whoever
does not receive the
Kingdom of God as
a child shall not
enter it.

Deut 30:6-20: Those who love
the Lord with all their heart
will live and possess the
land. Israelites given a

Mk 10:17-26: Man came
to Jesus to learn how
he might inherit life
eternal. Could not

choice between life and death.

keep the requirements of the new contract.

Mk 10:26: "And they were greatly surprised, saying to themselves, 'Then who can be saved?'"

Mark's "Deuteronomy" was reasonably well organized, beginning with Deut 2 and continuing through Deut 30, with enough important contacts in the proper order to make the outline discernible. It is about two and a half chapters in length, smaller than Mark's "Leviticus" but larger than his "Numbers." The summary sentence that is typical for Mark was properly placed at the end of this division, which is better than Matthew's summary statement is now placed. The "Deuteronomy" section also ended at just the place where it was necessary for a "Joshua" section to begin.

Joshua

Josh 1:1-9: After the death of Moses, the Lord reaffirmed his promise of the land to the people of Israel. Those who kept the law would

prosper.

Mk 10:28-34: Jesus reassured the disciples that those who had made sacrifices for the sake of the gospel and of Jesus would be amply repaid, both in this age and in the next. Jesus told of his imminent death.

Josh 1:10-18: Families of Reuben, Gad, and half of the Manasseh allowed to stay in Transjordan, but men required

to fight with the rest.

Mk 10:35-45: Brothers asked for favored positions. Jesus gave them opportunities to suffer and serve with the rest.

Josh 2:1-21: At Jericho Rahab asked spies for mercy for herself and her family in exchange for the trust she had in them.

Mk 10:46-52: Blind Bartimaeus cried out for mercy. Because of of this faith, Jesus restored his sight.

Josh 5:10-12: Before entering Jericho, Israelites celebrated the first Passover.

Mk 11:1-7: Jesus sent two messengers to make preparations for Passover and entrance into Jerusalem.

Josh 6:1-21: People marched around Jericho in procession and at the right time shouted. Then the walls fell down, and they entered and took the city.

Mk 11:7-11: Jesus entered the city of Jerusalem in procession as those nearby shouted.

Josh 6:26: Joshua cursed anyone who rebuilt the city of Jericho.

Mk 11:12-14: Jesus cursed the fig tree that it might never bear fruit again.

Josh 7:6-26: Joshua cleansed the Israelites from the sin of stealing the devoted booty destroying Achan, his family, and their possessions.

Mk 11: 15-17: Jesus cleansed the temple by overturning the tables of the money changers. The temple had become a cave of brigands.

Mk 11:18: "Now the chief priests and scribes heard, and they began to look for a way to destroy him, because they were afraid of him, for all the crowd was surprised at his teaching."

Conclusion. Fig tree dried up. Jesus told his disciples that if they had faith nothing was impossible for them. Encouragement to pray and forgive.

This appears to be a complete book, with the suitable summaries at the proper places to divide the book into units like a Hexateuch. The concluding encouragement to pray and forgive is a far more likely ending than the sentence concluding Mk 16:8: ". . . for they were afraid." Furthermore the passage which continues appears to be a second ending: "And they came again into Jerusalem."[8] It is possible that the Gospel of Mark once ended at this point and was later extended so that its ending would concur with the ending of Matthew's gospel and to include some teaching material in between the ending of Mark and the Matthaean ending of Mark. This teaching material in chapter twelve was not included in the parallel Markan passages to Matthew that included them.

The Joshua section of Mark begins at about the corresponding place in the outline of the Gospel as the "Joshua" section of Matthew does, but the parallels are not the same. Whereas Matthew has a feast to correspond to the Passover meal in "Joshua," Mark has the first reference to preparation for the Passover. Whereas in Matthew the two messengers sent correspond to the two spies in Joshua, Mark mentioned the two

messengers but not at a place to correspond to the two
spies. Instead, blind Bartemaeus begging for mercy
corresponds to Rahab asking for mercy. If Joshua were
concluded here and Mark were concluded here, the correspondence between Mark and the HS Hexateuch would be
unusually striking with proper conclusions at the
right places. This would be a fitting place to end the
gospel, even though Joshua does not end there. Since
Jesus was crucified shortly after his entrance into
Jerusalem and a Passover with his disciples, the Gospel of Mark may have intended only to follow Joshua
past the point of his clear entrance into the promised
land. The "Genesis" section of Mark was very small,
indicating little interest in events prior to the Exodus, but including main events in the proper order
from the Exodus to the entrance to the promised land.
This used the books of Exodus, Leviticus, Numbers,
Deuteronomy, and the first part of the Book of Joshua.

If Mark 12 was a later addition, then it was
apparently added with some understanding of the continuity needed to complete a gospel as the following
parallels show:

Josh 8:1-29: Joshua and the Israelites again went up to attack Ai. This time they captured it.	Mk 11:27-33: Jesus and the disciples again entered Jerusalem. There was a conflict with the chief priests and scribes. Jesus had the last word.
Josh 8:30-35: Joshua built an altar and offered sacri-fices.	Mk 12:1: Parable of a man who built a wine-press, tower, etc.
Josh 9:1-27: Gibeonites asked terms of peace from Joshua and he received them because they lied. He finally decreed that they would be hewers of wood and drawers of water, be-cause of their deception.	Mk 12:2-12: The te-nants rebelled and killed those sent to collect the rent.
Josh 10:1-12:23: Conflicts with many kings who tried to trap Joshua.	Mk 12:13-27: Conflicts with various political and religious groups that tried to trap Jesus in his talk.

Although there is some apparent continuity with the Gospel of Mark up to chapter 12, the parallels are not so apt. The first eleven chapters of Mark are mainly an account of actions with only notations that Jesus was also teaching all the while. Since Joshua is principally a book of action, its parallels in the teaching material of chapter 12 must be found in the activity described in the teaching. There were seventeen miracles in Mk 1:1-11, but none in the rest of the gospel. Daube has suggested that Mark 12 was originally a separate unit that was first used on Passover eve.[9] This hypothesis further explains the character of Mk 12 in contrast to Mk 1-11. If this were once a separate liturgical unit, containing many of the teachings of the Gospel of Matthew which the Gospel of Mark did not have, perhaps a later editor found it to be a suitable addition to improve the Gospel of Mark so as to make it more like Matthew. Further support for this addition is the rest of the Gospel of Mark which now parallels the Gospel of Matthew quite well, and consequently also parallels the end of the Book of Joshua.

Josh 13:1-19:51: Gathering of tribes and apportionment of the inheritance.

Mk 13:26:27: Son of man with angels to gather in the elect from the four corners of the earth.

Josh 24:1-26: Renewal of the contract in Joshua's

farewell speech.

Mk 14:24: Jesus' inauguration of the new contract in his farewell speech.

Josh 24:29-30: Death of Joshua.

Mk 14:43-15:39: Trial and death of Jesus (Joshua).

Josh 24:32: Bones of Joseph buried at Shechem on land bought for a hundred coins.

Mk 15:42-46: Body given to Joseph of Arimathea for burial.

SUMMARY

The "second ending" of Mark, which Daube thought included an early Passover haggadah, starts at a likely position to continue the pattern of Joshua. As Joshua <u>again</u> went up to take Ai, so Jesus <u>again</u> entered Jerusalem. From that point, however, until the renewal of the contract in Joshua 24, which corres-

ponds to the inauguration of the new contract in Mk
14:24, the correspondence is strained. This further
confirms the suggestion that Mark once ended with Mk
11:26, following Joshua through Josh 7.

The section in Joshua from 12:1-22:34 includes
a list of the kings Joshua captured, a list of tribes
and families, the division of the land, and establishment of cities of refuge and cities for Levites--not
very exciting material to imitate. Perhaps an editor
later tried to improve Mark by adding a Passover haggadah and using material in Matthew for a conclusion.
This would fill in a deficit of teaching in Mark that
the editor apparently thought existed. It would also
make Mark more like Matthew, so that the witnesses
would seem to be in greater agreement. The editor,
however, was also acquainted with the hexateuchal outline for a gospel, so that he added to the Gospel of
Mark in such a way as to complete the Book of Joshua
at the same time he made the improvements he believed
to be necessary. In relationship to the HS Hexateuch,
the Gospel of Mark is divided as follows:

1.   Genesis--Mk 1:1-3

2.   Exodus--Mk 1:4-21, plus: "And they were sur-
                             prised at his teach-
                             ing, for he taught
                             them as one who had
                             authority and not as
                             their scribes."[10]

3.   Leviticus--Mk 1:23-5:43, plus: "And he went
                             from there and came
                             to his fatherland,
                             and his disciples fol-
                             lowed him,2) and,
                             since it was on the
                             Sabbath, he began to
                             teach in the syna-
                             gogue, and the many,
                             when they heard were
                             surprised . . ."[11]

4.   Numbers--Mk 6:7-7:36, plus: "And they were very
                             much surprised, say-
                             ing, 'He did every-
                             thing well; he makes
                             the deaf hear and the
                             dumb speak.'"[12]

5. Deuteronomy--Mk 8:1-10:26, plus: "And they were
                                     very much surprised,
                                     saying to themselves,
                                     'Then who can be
                                     saved?'"[13]

6. Joshua--Mk 10:28-11:18, plus: "Now the chief
                                     priests and scribes
                                     heard, and they began
                                     to search for a way
                                     to destroy him, for
                                     all the crowd was
                                     surprised at his
                                     teaching.[14]

         Conclusion: Mk 11:19-26.
         Second ending of "Joshua":   a) Mk 12:1-44:
                                          Passover
                                          haggadah.
                                       b) Mk 13:1-
                                          15-46:
                                          Matthaean
                                          ending.

         Resurrection account beyond the Hexateuch:
                                          Mk 16:1-8

     The compressed and composite nature of Mark 13
is well known.[15] This 37 verse chapter parallels only
the first part of Matthew's discourse.[16] Matt 4:1-4
parallels Mk 13:1-4. Mark's conclusion, "When will be
the end (synteleisthai) of all these things?" is secondary to Matthew's, "What is the sign of your appearance and the end of the age (synteleias tou aiônos)?[17] Mk 13:4 has the only use in the Gospel of Mark
of the verb syntelein, whereas Matthew used the idiom,
synteleias tou aiônos, five times in his gospel. Mark
13:5-8 is a distilled version of Matt 24:4-13; Mk
13:10 parallels Matt 24:14, but Mk 13:9-13 forms a
poetic stanza for which the entire poem occurs in Matt
10:8-22. Mk 13:14-32 again parallels Matt 24:15-36
with quite reasonable consistency, but Mark's ending[18]
of the discourse has compressed into one parable the
elements of two in Matthew, which there required
twelve verses[19] plus an introduction.[20]

     Add to this the Passover haggadah of Mk 12 and
the ending[21] patterned after Matthew's ending, and
there is evidently the work of an editor who wished to
improve Mark by including much of the teaching material which Mark had omitted. Using Matthew as his

source, he added to the gospel without interrupting it internally. Hence the unity of Mk 1:1-11:18 is clear. But since his additions had to be put at the end in such a way as to complete a "Joshua," he was limited. Therefore he had to compress his material in the way his work reveals. The secondary nature of his material has convinced many scholars that "Mark" used "Matthew." This may or may not be true, but the secondary nature of Mk 12:1 ff. reflects the work of a later editor and not the work of the author of the gospel itself.

Although Mark, like Matthew, has five summary sentences, they have been placed in different positions in the outline of the material presented, as the following chart shows:

Mark's Summaries	Matthew's Parallels	Matthew's Summaries
1. Mk 1:22	Matt 7:28	Matt 7:28
2. Mk 6:2	Matt 13:53-54	Matt 11:1
3. Mk 7:37	Matt 15:31	Matt 13:53-54
4. Mk 10:26	Matt 19:25	Matt 19:1
5. Mk 11:18	After Matt 21:13 (see Matt 22:33)	Matt 26:1

The summary of Mark's "Exodus" coincides with Matthew's "Exodus," but the summary of Mark's "Leviticus" coincides with Matthew's "Numbers." Mark's "Numbers" section concludes with a Matthaean parallel almost two chapters beyond Matthew's summary. Mark's summary of "Deuteronomy" is as follows: "And they were very much surprised, saying to themselves, 'Then who can be saved?'"[22] Its parallel in Matthew is: "After they had heard, the disciples were very much surprised, saying, 'Who, then, can be saved?'"[23] The "Deuteronomy" section of Matthew did not really end with 18:35, but continued until Matt 20:17. Of the material between Matt 18:35 and 20:16, Matt 19:10-12 and 20:1-16 are unique to Matthew. The rest has basic parallels with the Gospel of Mark. It may be that the ending of Matthew was at one time closer to that of the Markan parallel at Matt 19:25, and that Matt 20:1-16 was added later.

The Markan parallel to Matt 26:1 would be Mk 14:1, which gives no hint of a summary. This would be after the little apocalypse.[24] This is not a suitable place to end either of the gospels. It is difficult to account for the possibilities that brought about the changes and apparent dislocation of the Matthaean summary, unless it was altered by attraction to a similar quotation in Joshua before the end of the Book of Joshua. The attraction of the summaries to one another is quite obvious. In addition to parallel expressions,[25] Matt 7:28 and Matt 13:53-54 have combined both the notations that Jesus had finished something and that the audience was astonished. Either Mark, starting with Matt 7:28, picked up the last clause and used it alone for the rest of his summaries, or Matthew, noting the astonishment expressed in Mk 1:22, added to the statement that the audience was surprised, a suitable observation after noting that Jesus had finished teaching all these things.

The divisions in the Gospel of Mark are better marked by summary statements than are the hexateuchal divisions in the Gospel of Matthew, who also has summary statements. If Mark used Matthew as a source, which seems more probable than vice versa, he probably employed the Gospel of Matthew in a pre-revised form and took his clue for the positions of the summary statements from Matthew. If the dependence were otherwise, then Matthew or his later reviser may have arranged his summary sentences to make room for additional material which he included.

Both gospel writers used five similar transition sentences. Both also showed good signs of having tried to imitate a pattern of the Hexateuch, even though their divisions were set in different places because their material was organized somewhat differently. It could not have been that one of the gospels imitated the other and accidentally wrote a book that fell into a hexateuchal pattern without the author's intention or awareness. This means that both gospel writers were writing with a certain understood design, which each followed even when it did not agree in order with the other gospel. Mark's interest in activity rather than teaching was shown by the size and nature of the sections he devoted to "Leviticus," "Numbers," and "Deuteronomy" in comparison to his "Exodus."

The suggestion that the Gospel of Mark once ended at 11:26 is further supported by the seventeen miracle stories in the first eleven chapters with none to follow and the extensive teaching material in chapters 12-15. In chapters 1-11, Mark reported many times that Jesus taught, but produced a proportionately small amount of teaching. This further suggests that the last five chapters were added by a later hand in imitation of the Gospel of Matthew. Because Matthew followed a hexateuchal pattern, the "second ending" of Mark also followed a "Joshua" in a rather rough way, but the author or editor who added this last section may not have been aware of the technical literary form required.

Both gospels seem to have supplemented their parallels from the Egyptian cycle with parallels from Second Isaiah's cycle. This is not as much out of order as it would seem initially. Since Jews believed that time moved in cycles and that the Babylonian captivity and exodus was simply a recurrence of the Egyptian captivity and exodus, it was considered proper to take data from one cycle to fill in lacunae in another cycle. Another example of this phenomenon occurs in Mekilta.[26] Here the midrashic author, while commenting on Exod 13:22: The Lord went before them during the day, concluded that when the Israelites left Egypt, there were clouds that raised the depressions and lowered the elevations on the way. His proof for this came from Isa 40:4: "Every valley shall be filled in and every mountain and hill shall be graded down; the rugged places will be leveled off and the rough places, smoothed out." The author of this midrash was not confused into thinking that Second Isaiah was referring to the exodus from Egypt rather than from Babylon. He just believed that if it had happened for the one deliverance it must have happened for the other. In a similar way Irenaeus held that since Jesus was the new Adam scholars could fill in unknown details about Adam from the known facts about Jesus. For example Irenaeus reasoned that Adam must have died on the day before the Sabbath, since he was the type for which Jesus was the antitype, and Jesus died on the day before the Sabbath.[27]

The author of Mark evidently reasoned in the same way that the rabbis, church fathers, and others of that age reasoned, believing that history repeats itself, systematically, and probably cyclically. When the gospel writers found parallels from Second Isaiah or Trito Isaiah to fill in lacunae not supplied by the Hexateuch, they were following the same kind of logic. This was particularly true of Mark, as other scholars have noticed. These scholars held that Mark was upholding suffering servant theology against some other kind of competing theology.[28] To do this, he quoted from Second Isaiah in appropriate places in the Gospel of Mark. In this way he filled in lacunae in the gospel form.

In Matthew and Mark no strain was required to show the traces of a Hexateuch. Revisions of the gospels may have blurred some divisions a bit, but not enough to destroy the outline completely. Next will be examined the Gospel of Luke to learn if it also follows a hexateuchal pattern.

ENDNOTES

1. Farrer, St. Matthew, pp. 193-94.
2. Ibid., p. 187.
3. Ibid., p. 187.
4. 1 Cor 10:11.
5. For the relationship between Isa 57-59 on Mk 2:10-3:6, see J. W. Doeve, Jewish Hermeneutic and the Synoptic Gospels (Assen, [1954]), pp. 203-04.
6. There is no real parallel in Leviticus for Mk 4:35-41. In Second Isaiah are parallels only to the extent that all of these show mastery over nature.
7. Mk 3:13-19.
8. Mk 11:27.
9. D. Daube, "The Earliest Structure of the Gospels," NTS 5 (1958/59):174-87.
10. Mk 1:22.
11. Mk 6:1-2.
12. Mk 7:37.
13. Mk 10:26.
14. Mk 11:18. C. H. Dodd, New Testament Studies (Manchester, c1954), studied the list of editorial summaries in the Gospel of Mark noted earlier by K. L. Schmidt, Der Rahmen der Geschichte Jesu: Mk 1:14-15, 21-22, 39; 2:13; 3:7b-19; 4:33-34; 6:7, 12-13; 6:30. Dodd noticed in these summaries, put together "a perspicuous outline of the Galilean ministry, forming a framework into which the separate pictures are set" (p. 8). Therefore Dodd suggested that the editor had in his possession both a collection of pictures and a frame in which to fit them and that he was required to fit the pictures into an already traditional frame. For that reason the editor's success was less than complete (p. 9-11).

Of Schmidt's summaries, only one, Mk 1:22, is the same as the summaries offered here. Although Schmidt's summaries used by Dodd included only Mk 1:1-6:30, the hexateuchal outline indicates also Mk 6:12 in this section. Dodd's suggestion of a previously structured outline is not exactly the solution offered here for the whole gospel section, Mk 1:1-11:18; but it seems likely that there is an understood six-fold division necessary at which points summaries would be in order.

D. E. Nineham, "The Order of Events in St. Mark's Gospel--an Examination of Dr. Dodd's Hypothesis," Studies in the Gospels, has adequately undercut every support for Dodd's hypothesis that the early church preserved an outline of Jesus's life which was the outline on which Mark constructed his Gospel.
15. B. C. Butler, The Originality of St. Matthew (Cambridge, 1951), pp. 76-85.

16.   Matt 24:1-26:1.
17.   Matt 24:4.
18.   Mk 13:33-37.
19.   Matt 24:45-25:6.
20.   Matt 24:37-44.
21.   Mk 14:1-15:46.
22.   Mk 10:26.
23.   Matt 19:25.
24.   Mk 13 and Matt 24-25.
25.   Matt 19:25 and Mk 10:26.
26.   Mek, Beshallah 1:178-92.
27.   Adv. Haer. 5:23, PG 1185B-C.
28.   So T. R. W. Longstaff, "Crisis and Christology: the
Theology of Mark," W. R. Farmer (ed.), New Synoptic Studies
(Macon, c1983):373-92, quoting also P. J. Achtemeier, Mark
(Philadelphia, 1975), pp. 41, 47, 99 and T. J. Weeden, Mark--
Traditions in Conflict (Philadelphia, 1971), pp. 52, 62, 160-
63.

CHAPTER FOUR

LUKE AND JEWISH LITERATURE

INTRODUCTION

Although Luke has been called a gospel and classified as a gospel in the canon, it does not begin as if it were the imitation of a Hexateuch. Instead, it begins as a letter to Theophilus, in which the author said that he was setting in order a written report of the things that had been fulfilled.[1] Since the author of this introduction admitted that many before him had produced materials reporting historical data about Jesus, it is possible that he himself was not primarily trying to compose a gospel but rather to report what could be known about Jesus, utilizing gospels and other sources available to him. If so, he may have used a gospel as the basis of his work which might still be traced in the canonical document. The search for such a gospel will be made in the following examination.

The story that begins with Lk 1:5 and continues to 3:22 is more Semitic in style and more dependent upon HS quotations than most of the Gospel of Luke. It really begins before the beginning of the Gospel. This section was probably added by the editor who wrote to Theophilus and wanted to include everything important and to organize it all into a logical sequence. Hence the birth narrative of John the Baptist must be a preamble to that of Jesus. The story of these two births was probably already composed and in some literary document at the time the editor wrote, so that he accepted this document that started from the beginning and continued until John had baptized Jesus before he followed the order of the gospel. After that story, however, the gospel followed in the hexateuchal order.

Genesis

Gen 1:5Ø: Beginning of creation, man (Adam) and his successors down to	Lk 3:23-38: The beginning of Jesus' ministry together with a list of his progenitors from Joseph back to Adam.
Joseph son of Jacob.	

This is not an extensive Book of Genesis, but neither were the divisions allotted to Genesis in Matthew and especially Mark. Evidently the real point of interest in a gospel was from the exodus until the entrance into the promised land in the HS, paralleled by the ministry of Jesus until the entrance into Jerusalem and the death of Jesus in the NT. Without any transition sentence the "Exodus" division began at Lk 4:1.

Exodus

Exod 15:22: Moses led Israel away from the Red Sea, and they went into the Wilderness of Shur.

Lk 4:1: Jesus turned away from the Jordan led by the Spirit into the wilderness.

Exod 16:1-34:35: The Israelites wandered in the wilderness, tempting the Lord by complaining for lack of food and water, worshipping the golden calf, and Moses' request to see God to be sure of his promise. God put him in a cleft of the rock and covered him with his hand.

Lk 4:1-13: The Lord was tempted by the devil in the wilderness forty days. He was tempted to produce bread from stone, worship Satan, and hurl himself down from a pinnacle of the temple to be sure that God would care for him.

Exod 24:7: Moses read the Book of the Contract to the people.

Lk 4:16-30: Jesus read from Isaiah 61:1-2. in synagogue in Nazareth.

Lk 4:31-32: "And he went down into Capernaum, a city in Galilee, and he was teaching them on the Sabbath, and they were surprised at his teaching, because his word was with authority."

Jesus's homecoming as it was reported in Luke is clearly a midrash on the reports given in Matt 13:53-58 or Mk 6:1-6, both of which are expanded chreias. Luke alone mentioned Nazareth and interpreted "teaching" to mean reading scripture and expounding on the text. Since Luke has no "Sermon on the Mount," and since Jesus' sermon follows the temptations, he may have intended this sermon to be the antitype for Moses' reading of the commandments after he had come down from the mountain. This sermon holds the same position, sequentially, as Matthew's Sermon on the Mount. Luke's report of the temptations of Jesus are

87

in a different order from those of Matthew, but they
concur with the order of temptations of Moses and the
Israelites in the wilderness. Luke's "Exodus" section
is quite small, because he did not include a mountain
scene to parallel the giving of the law on Mount Sinai. Jesus's reading of scripture and delivering a
sermon at Nazareth seems to have been the Lukan equivalent of Moses's giving of the law. Luke's summary was
much like that of Mark except that it followed a sentence telling of his geographical transfer of positions. Since the baptism of Jesus was covered in the
birth and development stories of John and Jesus, there
is no Exodus parallel to the crossing of the Red Sea.
Jesus' turning away from the Jordan, however, was the
first place in Exodus that it was possible to report
on "Exodus" after the crossing. This Luke did.

Leviticus

Lev 5:1-6: Uncleanness from
touching and means for forgiveness.

Lk 4:33-37: Jesus
healed a man with an
unclean spirit by
driving out the
spirit.

Lk 4:40-41: Jesus
touched many and
healed them by
driving out the
demons.

Lev 6:8-10:20: Instructions
given to Aaron and sons;
two sons
broke the rules and
were consumed.

Lk 5:1-11: Call of
disciples and direc-
tions given. Peter
confessed himself to
be sinful.

Lev 13-14: Rules for detect-
ing and cleansing from
leprosy.

Lk 5:11-16: Jesus
cleansed a man who
was full of leprosy
and ordered him to
fulfill the rules of
Leviticus.

Lev 16:1-34: Rules for obtaining forgiveness of sins
on the Day of Atonement. Involves repentance and afflic-
tion of their souls.

Lk 5:17-26: Jesus
healed a paralytic and
enabled him to walk by
forgiveness of his
sins.

Lk 5:27-35: Jesus

	called Levi, a tax collector, to be his disciple. Jesus ate in Levi's house. He called sinners to repentance. Jesus and disciples did not fast.
Lev 19:1-37: Society rules involve keeping Sabbaths.	Lk 6:1-11: Jesus' disciples picked grain on the Sabbath. Jesus healed a man with a withered hand on the Sabbath.
Lev 23:1-25:55: Sabbaths in relationship to other feasts, Sabbath years, and Jubilee years.	
Lev 26:1-46: Blessings promised for those who keep the contract and the curses for those who break it.	Lk 6:17-26: Beatitudes and woes for people of varying qualities.

There is nothing in the last chapter of Leviticus that has a striking resemblance to the continuing section in Luke, so it appears as if the Leviticus division is over. The change from Leviticus is not sharp. There is no summarizing sentence or clear transfer of topics.

Numbers

Num 5:1-4: Treatment of a person who had become unclean by touching a dead body.	Lk 7:11-17: Jesus raised and brought to life the dead son of the widow of Nain by touching him.
Num 11:1-35: Nothing could satisfy the Israelites.	Lk 7:24-35: Neither John nor Jesus could please the Israelites.
Num 12:1-16: Miriam rebelled, was smitten by leprosy, and healed because of Moses' intercession.	Lk 7:36-50: Woman who was a sinner anointed Jesus' feet. Her sins were forgiven.
Num 13:1-20: Twelve spies	Lk 9:1-5: Twelve

appointed to search out the land before the invasion.

disciples appointed to proclaim the Kingdom of God.

Num 13:21-33: Twelve spies returned and made a report; some good and some bad. Feared the Canaanites.

Lk 9:7-10: Twelve returned and told what they did. Herod a threat. He had beheaded John the Baptist.

Num 14:20-35: Adults refused admission into the land. Children would enter it after the adults had died.

Lk 9:46-48: Those who received children in Christ's name received Christ.

Num 16:1-50: Korah led a rebellion. He and his party were swallowed up. Moses stood between the living and the dead.

Luke 9:60-62: The dead were to bury their own dead. No one who put his hand to the plow and looked back was fit for the Kingdom of God.

The above outline shows some parallels between this Lukan section and the Book of Numbers, but there are other parallels that would not fit into the proper sequence:

Num 9:1-14: Passover.

Lk 9:12-17: Feeding the multitide.

Num 9:15-23: Cloud over the tabernacle continually.

Lk 9:28-36: Mount of Transfiguration; voice from a cloud.[2]

Num 11:14: Moses: "I am not

able to carry this people alone."

Lk 9:37-43: Boy possessed by unclean spirit; Jesus: "How long will I be with you?"

Num 11:26: Joshua asked Moses to forbid Eldad and Medad from

prophesying. Moses allowed it.

Lk 9:29-50: John forbade others to cast out demons in Jesus' name. Jesus permitted it.

There are enough parallels out of order to suggest that this was once a well-organized unit that had been later revised without the same interest in maintaining hexateuchal unity and order. This further

points to an editor who added the salutation, the
birth narratives, and some other Jewish units. When he
did this, this editor destroyed the gospel form. The
Book of Deuteronomy, however, has been well preserved.
This has been shown by Evans,[3] whose parallels are
summarized as follows, with only one addition.[4]

Deuteronomy

Deut 1: Moses led from Horeb.	Lk 10:1-3, 17-20: Jesus led from Mount of Transfiguration.
Sent twelve spies who reported	He sent seventy in addition to the twelve.
that the land was fruitful.	The harvest was abundant.
Deut 2:3-22: Og rejected the	Lk 10:4-16: Wipe the dust off your feet.
embassy and was destroyed.	Woe to Chorazin, Bethsaida, and Capernaum.
Deut 3:23-40: Moses prayed.	Lk 10:21-24: Jesus prayed. Things concealed yet to be revealed to babes.
Entry into promised land refused.	
Deut 5-6: The Decalog.	Lk 10:25-27: "What is written in the law?"
Deut 7: Destroy the foreigner;	Lk 10:29-37: The parable of the good Samaritan who shows mercy.
show no mercy on him.	
Deut 8:1-3: Man does not live by bread alone.	Lk 10:38-42: Mary not busied with food.
Deut 8:1: God deals with	Lk: 11:1-13: The Lord's prayer. God is much better than a father.
Israel as a father.	
Deut 9:1-10:11: Israel a stubborn people.	Lk 11:14-26: The people do not recognize the signs of the the kingdom.

Deut 10:12-11:32: Love God

with whole heart. Israel's
eyes have seen great wonders.

Deut 12:1-6: Clean and
unclean.

Deut 12:17 ff.: Rejoice with
wealth before God.

Deut 13:1-11: Death upon any
one who leads Israel to other

Gods. Do not be enticed by
family.

Deut 13:12 ff.: Communal destruction for communal
apostasy.

Deut 14:28: Feed the poor
with the tithe.

Deut 15:1-8: Release from
debt and slavery.

Deut 16:1-17:7: Rules for
feasts at Jerusalem.

Deut 17:8-18: Judges must not
be perverted. Support for the
priests and Levites.

Deut 20: How to be excused
from holy war. Making peace
and destruction.

Deut 21:15-22:4: Father and
son. Restoration of the lost.
A prodigal
son shall be stoned.

Deut 23:15-24:4: A runaway

Lk 11:27-36: Blessed
are they who keep the
word of God. If the
eye is evil, the whole
body is dark.

Lk 11:37-12:12: Clean
and unclean.

Lk 12:13-34: Rich
toward God.

Lk 12:35-53: Faith-
fulness of the Lord's
stewards. A family
will be divided by
Christ.

Lk 12:54-13:5: Commu-
nal judgment and re-
pentance.

Lk 13:6-9: The un-
fruitful vineyard.

Lk 13:10-21: Jesus
heals on the Sabbath.

Lk 13:22-35: Enter by
the narrow gate. Jeru-
salem is the place
where the prophets are
sacrificed.

Lk 14:1-14: Jesus
dined with a Pharisee.
The poor should be
invited to feasts.

Lk 14:15-35: No excuse
for not serving the
kingdom. Counting the
cost before building
or fighting.

Lk 15: Parables of
lost and found. For-
giveness of the
prodigal son.

Lk 16:1-18: The par-

slave shall not be oppressed. Divorce rules.	able of the unjust steward. Divorce and and adultery.
Deut 24:6-25:3: Injunctions against oppressive treatment of the poor. Take heed of leprosy. Do not take the millstone as a pledge. The judges shall justify the righteous.	Lk 16:19-18:8: The vindication of the poor by God. Ten lepers healed. Better a millstone around the neck. God will vindicate his elect.
Deut 26: Praise, confession, and profession shall be cried aloud in the Lord's sanctuary.	Lk 18:9-14: The parable of the Pharisee and the tax collector, praying in the temple.

Luke has included no summary to the Deuteronomy section the way Mark did. Nonetheless, Luke's Deuteronomy division is the sharpest of all, showing parallels with the Hexateuch. Drury was impressed both with Farrer's discovery of a hexateuchal pattern in Matthew and with Evans's demonstration of the Deuteronomy section. For his part Drury argued that Luke used both Deuteronomy and Matthew while he composed the "travel narrative" of Luke.[5]

The last two items of Luke's "Deuteronomy" section could also find parallels in the Book of Joshua, because both the end of Deuteronomy and the beginning of Joshua deal with the situation around Jericho just before entering into the promised land. Hence the dividing line intended is rather hazy, but Joshua should begin at the entrance and at Jericho, so the division belongs in this general area.

Joshua

Josh 2:1-14: Rahab took side of the Israelites at Jericho. Will sacrifice the rest of the city for herself and family.	Lk 19:1-9: Zechariah joined Jesus's movement near Jericho. Was willing to give half of his money to atone for dishonesty and the rest to a group called "the poor."
Josh 1:1-9: Expectation of immediate reception of the kingdom.	Lk 19:10-12: Expectation of immediate reception of the

kingdom.

Josh 1:10-28: Organization of officers and assignment of duties.	Lk 19:13-26: Assignment of responsibilities to servants.
Josh 2:1-24: Two spies went to Jericho to prepare for Joshua's coming.	Lk 19:28-35: Two messengers sent ahead to prepare for Jesus' coming.
Josh 3:1-17: Israelites cross Jordan in parade.	Lk 19:36-38: Jesus and followers enter Jerusalem in parade.
Josh 4:1-24: Memorial of twelve stones set up.	Lk 19:39-40: Jesus said that if the disciples kept still the stones would cry out.[6]
Josh 5:1-9: Kings feared Joshua. Joshua circumcised children born in the wilderness.	Lk 20:1-8: Scribes, chief priests, and elders asked about the authority of Jesus. Replied in reference to the validity of John's baptism.
Josh 13:15: Joshua confronted the commander of the Lord's army and was humbled; became commander's servant.	Lk 20:9-18: Landlord and servants in the vineyard. Servants to be destroyed.
Josh 16-21: Divisions of the land so that each tribe received its fair share.	Lk 20:19-26: Consideration of the things that belong to Caesar and things that belong to God.
Josh 23: Joshua recounted the the way the Lord had fulfilled his promise. He warned that if Israelites did not keep the commandments, the Lord would drive them off the land.	Lk 21: Jesus warned the disciples not to wander. Describes hardships that lay in the future including the destruction of Jerusalem.
Josh 24:1-26: Joshua renewed the contract between the Lord and his people.	Lk 22:1-20: Last supper with his disciples inaugurated the new contract.

94

Josh 24:29-30: Death of Joshua.	Lk 22:47-23:49: Capture, trial, and death of Jesus.
Josh 24:32: Bones of Joseph buried in a newly bought tomb at Shechem.	Lk 23:50-56: Joseph of Arimathea buried the body of Jesus in a new tomb.

The "Joshua" section of Luke, like the same division of Matthew and the second ending of Mark, ended just before the resurrection account. Except for the lack of summary statements to show the ends of divisions, the prelude to Genesis, and the apparent reorganization of some of the material, especially in the "Numbers" section, Luke, like Mark and Matthew, preserved an account of the early events in the Christian faith following the pattern of the history of the children of Israel, with special emphasis on the events from the exodus until the entrance into the land. If Jesus' activity actually happened in the sequence that the synoptic gospels report then he consciously relived the experiences of his people in the earlier periods of the exodus from Egypt and the return of the captives from Babylon, but this seems too artificial to be true. It is more than likely that the events in the life of Jesus were organized into a literary form that was consciously patterned after the main events in the history of Israel, following the divisions in the Hexateuch.

The synoptic gospels may have had more than one revision since the original composition, in just the same way that the Rule of the Community (1QS) shows signs of revision. This seems the normal development for a community's rule book. New needs require new additions or interpretations. The basic pattern of Matthew and Luke continue to be that of a Hexateuch. Luke seems to be a book that was based on a gospel but which has been revised. The revising editor wrote for Theophilus a "life of Jesus" based on a gospel that was available to him together with other sources. At that time he might have removed some of the transition sentences that once marked the divisions of the "Hexateuch," added a prologue to the gospel so that he could include as much as could be known about Jesus, and reorganized some of the material within the gospel. This would have enabled him to introduce some additional teachings, not originally in the gospel, which provided the basis for his "life of Jesus" in an epistle form.

95

In previous chapters the HS was shown to be very influential in forming the guidelines for faith and practice of later Jews and Christians. This chapter has shown that the Hexateuch was sufficiently important to early Christians for them to pattern some of their major documents after it. Farrer was correct in noting that the addition of the "Joshua" section to a gospel was probably done to show Jesus, not only as the new Moses, but also as the new Joshua. This was partly suggested by the name, Joshua, which is translated "Jesus" in Greek.

The Pentateuch was the central unit in NT times, but Joshua was originally written to be the final book of the Torah, making the canonical unit a Hexateuch rather than a Pentateuch. This is evident from the inclusio fashion by which it is organized in relationship to Genesis. In Genesis Abraham began by traveling to the land which was promised to him and his children. He entered the promised land at Shechem. It was not only to Abraham that God made the promise of the land, but it was with Abraham that God first entered into a contract relationship. Joshua concludes after the promise given to Abraham had been fulfilled; the tribes had been established on the land; and the children of Abraham were gathered again at Shechem to recite a creed, starting with Abraham's beginning experience with God and the renewal of the contract to accept the God of Abraham and observe his commandments. It concludes on the promised land with a recital of God's saving acts and with the people and Joshua accepting the contract with the Lord at Shechem-- the very place where Abraham entered the promised land.[7]

Since Joshua included the conquest of Canaan, it is easy to understand why it was included to make a Hexateuch of the canon. The Samaritans probably omitted it, because it was not spoken by Moses, and Jews had to recognize that it was not composed by Moses or any of the proved prophets. Like Genesis, it was not clearly the word of God and not as popular as Exodus, Numbers, and Deuteronomy. Both Genesis and Joshua were forced into the category of "law." It may have been the Mosaic and legal categories that separated Joshua from the "law," but Joshua continued to be a popular book, so it was no difficulty for a Christian gospel writer to reinclude it because of the name, Jesus, as an antitype of the old Jesus (Joshua). The Pentateuch continued to hold a very important place in Judaism--

not only in faith and practice, but also in formation of its later literature. This can be noted from several points of observation.

THE PENTATEUCH IN JUDAISM

Onkelos and the gospel. The Samaritans claimed the Pentateuch as the complete canon. The great majority of Philo's extensive writings are interpretations of the Pentateuch. Targum Onkelos, held by medieval rabbis to be the only targum to which sanctity applied, is a targum of the Pentateuch.[8] The name, Onkelos, has usually been believed to be a misspelling for Aquila (ʿaqylah),[9] a proselyte who worked to produce a more literal Greek translation of the HS than the LXX. Another possibility might be that)wnqlws was pointed ewanqelos to give a Hebrew spelling for the Greek word euaggelos.

The difficulty of spelling a Hebrew word that began with two successive vowel sounds is obvious. At best, only an approximation could be made. The Greek eu is sometimes used only to have the effect of a prosthetic alef when dealing with loan words, such as the Greek Euphrates for parat. Words like diatheke, docheion, and balniaria have been spelled in Hebrew dyyatheyqey,[10] dakeyn,[11] and balksary.[12] Since Aquila did not really work on a targum and since)onqelos does not really spell ʿaqylah, the possibility that the targum on the Pentateuch was once called a gospel might be worth consideration. The close relationship of the synoptic gospels to the Hexateuch supports the possibility that non-Christian Jews of NT times, who were looking for a new deliverance, also gave central attention to those books of the HS which told of the deliverance from Egypt, the wandering in the wilderness, and the preparation for entrance into the promised land.

Among the non-Christian Jews that anticipated a new deliverance were such leaders as Theudas who led a group of Jews to the river Jordan, assuring them that, like Joshua, he would divide the Jordan so that they could pass over on dry land.[13] Josephus reported other leaders to have attracted large numbers of Jews out to the wilderness where they promised to show signs (semeia) of deliverance.[14] One of these "false prophets" was an Egyptian who led a large group through the wilderness toward the Mount of Olives, from which point he said he could command the walls of Jerusalem to fall and provide an entrance so that he could overthrow the Romans.[15] Attempts made by Jewish leaders to imitate the events of the entrance into the promised land by Joshua and his followers show that Jews of that time were very much aware of the details leading up to the first conquest of Canaan and that they expected history to repeat itself.

Tannaitic midrashim. The Tannaitic midrashim consist of Mekilta, Sifra, and Sifre. These are early commentaries on the books of Exodus, Leviticus, Numbers, and Deuteronomy--all books related to the exodus and preparation for entrance into the promised land. Like the synoptic gospels, Tannaitic authors evidently were less interested in the Book of Genesis. After all, it was not written or spoken by Moses, God's apostle or legal agent. Like Joshua, its status as God's word could be questioned.

Also like the synoptic gospels, with the exception of Sifra which comments on every verse of Leviticus, these commentaries omitted many parts of each book while commenting on the passages each commentator believed central. Mekilta is a commentary on Exod 12:1-23:19; 31:12-17; and 35:1-3, omitting all the events in Egypt prior to the Passover,[16] warnings and promises,[17] acceptance of the book of the contract,[18] construction of the ark and tent of meeting,[19] the tabernacle,[20] materials and directions for Aaron's priestly function.[21] The commentary covers the text from the escape out of Egypt to the provision of the ten commandments and other rules at Mount Sinai,[22] and the rules for the Sabbath.[23] It was apparently composed to clarify the rules of ethics demanded of Israelites in relation to the exodus from Egypt. Rules for the priests and history of events in Egypt lay beyond the purpose of the commentator. The ten commandments were not only omitted in Mekilta, but also in Sifre on Deuteronomy.

Sifre on Numbers is very sketchy, compared to Sifra. Perhaps because the author thought they were less important than the parts on which he commented, the commentator or later editor failed to comment on statistical records, such as the numbering of the tribes and the tasks assigned to the Levites,[24] the lists of contributions given for the dedication of the altar,[25] details of names and census of Midian,[26] the boundaries of the land, and the officials appointed to divide it.[27] He also omitted material related to the priests, Levites, or tabernacle, such as the purification of the Levites,[28] the rebellion of the Levites and Aaron's vindication,[29] the description of the cloud over the tabernacle,[30] the prescription of ways to conduct appointed feasts,[31] and the establishment of cities for the Levites.[32]

This may reflect an anti-priestly Tendenz, or it may indicate an attempt to avoid repetition of material already commented on in Sifra. Also omitted were such uncomplimentary reports as Moses' complaint to the Lord, Israel's craving for meat, and the prophesying of Eldad and Medad;[33] the spying out of the land and the curse against those who tested the Lord,[34] the complaint of the Israelites at the water shortage, and their rejection by the Edomites.[35] Here might also be classed again Korah's rebellion and Aaron's vindication.[36] The curse against those who spied out the land[37] has its parallel in Deuteronomy, and received no comment from this commentator, probably because this was one of the records that did not show Israel in a good light, and so it was not "good news." Other events, understood to be historical, such as the capture of Arad, Ammon, and Bashan; the story of Balak and Balaam,[38] settling of Reuben, Gad, and half of Manassa, in Transjordan; and the outline of the journey from Egypt to Palestine,[39] were also omitted even though some of the events were only recorded in Numbers.

Sifre on Deuteronomy is more nearly complete than Sifre on Numbers, partially, perhaps, because Deuteronomy has more unparalleled text than Numbers. Like Sifre on Numbers, Sifre on Deuteronomy did not comment on the report of the spies, the curse, the journey through the wilderness to Palestine, preliminary battles, and the settlement of the two and a half tribes in Transjordan.[40] Also omitted are many of the admonitions to keep the commandments with the consequent rewards or punishments promised, as well as the doctrine of Israel's election. This omission included the ten commandments, also omitted in the Mekilta.[41] Some of these may have been excluded because the same themes were reported many times in the Book of Deuteronomy. Also excluded are details of kasher meat,[42] and most of Moses' farewell speech and exhortation.[43]

The editing done in Sifre on Deuteronomy shows the hand of an original author rather than a later editor who cut out certain portions. As in Sifre on Numbers, he omitted sections that disparaged the Israelites. This purpose is further confirmed by the invocation added as a conclusion to the entire Sifre: "I give thanks to you, O Lord, my God and the God of my fathers, that you have assigned my portion among those who dwell in the beth ha-midrash, etc. May it be approved before you that our hatred of [other] men not rise up against the views (lêb) of [other] men (ʾadam) and that the hatred of [other] men may not rise up against our views. And may our zeal not rise up against the views of [other] men and may the zeal of [other] men not rise up against our views. And may your Torah be our employment all the days of our lives, etc."

In both Numbers and Deuteronomy, Sifre omitted passages dealing with priests and Levites. An anti-priestly Tendenz seems evident in Sifre[44] where the benefits of the priesthood are tabulated, concluding with: "It was a great joy for Aaron on the day when there was cut for him a contract with offerings." Some of the editing was artfully done. For instance, the transfer from Deut 6:9 to Deut 10 allowed the content to continue coherently. The further construction of a sermon based on Deut 29:9 and 31:4 was done to keep the whole message unified without the pedantics of commenting on each verse. Although there is a great deal of repetition within the Tannaitic midrashim, parts of the text omitted were probably the result of an intention to avoid the kind of duplication found in the books of the Pentateuch and the synoptic gospels.

The Tannaitic midrashim were documents used to explain the teachings and events associated with the exodus and preparation to enter the promised land. Sifra is a complete commentary on Leviticus. Mekilta and Sifre represented the books of Exodus, Numbers, and Deuteronomy, even though the outlines of these books were rather sketchily followed with many omissions. This is very similar to the outlines in the synoptic gospels argued here as parallels to the hexateuchal books. The Book of Genesis, ignored by Tannaitic commentators, was given only a slight recognition in the synoptic gospels. The books of Leviticus for Mark and Deuteronomy for Luke were both proportionately more complete than the Book of Exodus in either gospel. But the order, division content, and organization of all three synoptic gospels show an intentional imitation of the organization of the Hexateuch related together with reports of plans for a new exodus in Second Isaiah.

This intrusion of Second or Trito Isaiah is not
out of order for this program. Rabbis frequently supplemented the events of one exodus with those of another. For example, Mekilta consciously related the
exodus from Egypt to the exodus of Abram from Ur of
the Chaldee and the exodus from Babylon. This was done
because they thought one exodus was an antitype of an
earlier exodus. Therefore, they must have been identical, from some points of view. The synoptic gospels
show the concentration of Christians in NT times on
previous deliverances. The literature developed was
closely related to other Jewish writings dealing with
HS literature in NT times.

Although these gospels had characteristics of
biographies, they were not just biographies of Jesus;
they were interpretations of a new deliverance from
slavery and a new restoration of the promised land to
a new people of God in fulfillment of promises made to
Abraham long before. By relating these anticipations
to the life and activity of Jesus, Christians developed a new literary form--the gospel, but it was not
out of character for Judaism. Like other experiences,
beliefs, and literary forms in Judaism it was coherent
with their well-known typology, cyclical time, and
centrality of the Torah. In many ways it was related
to the teachings of Philo, Onkelos, and the Tannaitic
midrashim.

1.   Lk 1:1.
2.   J. Manek, "The New Exodus in the Books of Luke," Nov 2 (1958):8-23, noted the reference to Jesus's "Exodus" from Jerusalem in Lk 9:31. From there concluded that Luke and Acts both considered the resurrection of Jesus to be an exodus.
3.   Evans, "The Central Section," pp. 42-50. B. Reicke, "Instruction and Discussion in the Travel Narrative," Studia Evangelica 1 (1959):206-16), has shown that Lk 10:1-18:14 is almost rhythmically balanced by alternative instruction and discussion. This is comparable to the teaching and exhortation of the Book of Deuteronomy.
4.   The last example: Deut 26 and Lk 18:9-14.
5.   J. Drury, Tradition and Design in Luke's Gospel (London, c1976), pp. 138-64.
6.   O. J. F. Seitz, "What Do These Stones Mean?" JBL 79 (1960):247-54.
7.   For the development of the Hexateuch, see G. Von Rad, The Problem of the Hexateuch, tr. E. W. T. Dicken (New York, c1966), pp. 1-93. For its early importance see J. Sanders, Torah and Canon (Philadelphia, c1972), pp. 25-27. He said, "We can be rather confident that at one point the Torah concluded with the Book of Joshua" (p. 26).
8.   See W. Bacher, "Targum," JE 12, p. 59.
9.   Ibid., pp. 58-59.
10. TShab. 8:13 (120); TBB 8:8 (409).
11. TKelim 5:7-8 (574-75).
12. TKelim 5:16 (80).
13   Ant 20.97.
14. Ant 20.167-68.
15. BJ 2.261-63.
16. Exod 1-11.
17. Exod 23:20-32.
18. Exod 24.
19. Exod 25.
20. Exod 26-27.
21. Exod 28:1-31:1.
22. Exod 12:1-23:19.
23. Exod 31:12-17; 35:1-3.
24. Num 1-4.
25. Num 7:19-83.
26. Num 31:25-54.
27. Num 34:1-29.
28. Num 8:5-23.
29. Num 16:1-17:13.
30. Num 9:15-23.
31. Num 29:1-11, 13-35.
32. Num 35:1-8.

33.   Num 10:11-28.
34.   Num 13:1-14:25.
35.   Num 20:1-29.
36.   Num 16:1-17:3.
37.   Num 13:1-14:45.
38.   Num 21:1-24:25.
39.   Num 32:1-33:56; Deut 1:1-3:29.
40.   Deut 4:1-6:3; 6:10-11:9.
41.   Deut 14:8-10; 15-19.
42.   Deut 29:11-31:13.
43.   Deut 32:1-43 (31:15-30).
44.   SNum 18:20; 39b #119.

CHAPTER FIVE

GOSPELS AND MIRACLE TRADITIONS

INTRODUCTION

After noting the close relationship between the synoptic gospels and the HS Hexateuch, even a hasty reading of the Fourth Gospel shows that it does not follow the same pattern. The book begins and ends like a gospel, but that is all. The prologue properly opens with "In the beginning" (en archê) exactly as Genesis does, and the Word that was present in God's creation[1] recalls the story of creation when God spoke and the creation took place.[2] Also in Genesis God's word brought about light and light in the firmament as well as life in the firmament and life on the land. John said that in this Word "was life, and life was light of men."[3] As in Genesis, this light shone in the darkness, and the darkness was not able to overpower it.[4] From the creation story in Genesis, the narrative immediately moves to Exodus themes: "The true light that lightens every man coming into the world"[5] recalls the burning bush that appeared to Moses.[6] The glory (doxa) that Christians observed was like the glory of the Lord (tên doxan kyriou) that appeared to the Israelites in the wilderness.[7] The claim that the Word had pitched its tent (eskênôsen) in the midst of the people[8] is a reminder of the sanctuary (miqdaš) in the wilderness at which place the Lord promised to dwell (šakan).[9] This tent evidently had a fire burning there all the time to show the Lord's real presence. At night the pillar of fire showed up; during the day time the smoke was more obvious than the fire. The pillar of cloud and fire was called the glory of the Lord which accompanied Israel in all of its journeys.

But that which began as a gospel did not continue as a gospel after the prologue until the beginning of the passion narratives at the end of the book.[10] In between is a collection of miracle stories that is organized according to no pentateuchal pattern but resembles closely the group of miracles of Elijah and Elisha reported in the Books of Kings. A series of comparisons will make this obvious:

ELIJAH, ELISHA, AND JESUS

Elisha Parallels	Miracles of Elijah	Miracles of Elisha
2	i. Stopped rain.[11]	1. Divided waters of the Jordan.[12]
5, 8, 9	ii. Provided widow's meal and oil.[13]	2. Purified water at Jericho.[14]
6, 7, 10, 14	iii. Revived widow's son.[15]	3. Called bears to destroy 42 boys.[16]
4	iv. Called down fire from heaven.[17]	4. Filled stream bed with water.[18]
3, 11, 13	v. Fire consumed Ahaziah's soldiers.[19]	5. Filled son of prophet's oil jars.[20]
	vi. Fire consumed Ahaziah's soldiers.[21]	6. Provided son for Shunamite woman.[22]
	vii. Elijah parted waters of Jordan.[23]	7. Revived Shunamite's son.[24]
		8. Purified stew.[25]
		9. Multiplied loaves.[26]
		10. Cured commander's leprosy.[27]
		11. Afflicted Gehazi with leprosy.[28]
		12. Made ax head float.[29]
		13. Struck Syrians with blindness.[30]
		14. Man revived who touched Elisha's bones.[31]

When Elisha was granted a double portion of Elijah's spirit,[32] he evidently was given power to perform twice as many miracles as Elijah,[33] and they were of the same nature. Elijah performed seven miracles, Elisha, fourteen, and Jesus, according to the Fourth Gospel, performed seven signs, which were very similar to those of the Israelite prophets, except that Jesus was credited with more healing miracles and none of the destructive miracles.

Elijah Parallel	Elisha Parallel	Signs of Jesus
ii.	2, 4, 5, 8	1. Changed water to wine.[34]
	10	2. Healed centurion's son.[35]
		3. Healed lame man at pool.[36]
ii.	9	4. Multiplied loaves.[37]
vii.	1, 2	5. Walked on water.[38]
	13	6. Healed blind beggar at Pool of Siloam.[39]
ii.	7, 14	7. Raised Lazarus.[40]

The signs of Jesus in the Fourth Gospel have been patterned intentionally after the miracles of Elijah and Elisha. This is evident from a comparison of themes and words of the miracle stories involved.

THE WEDDING AT CANA

Jesus[41]	Elijah[42]	Elisha[43]
1. Woman recognized need; host unable to fulfill hospitality obligation.	Woman in need; embarrassed by hospitality obligation.	Woman in need; unable to meet obligation of creditor.
2. Asked Jesus for help.		Asked Elisha for help.
3. Response seemed unreasonable: "What have you to do with me?"	Request seemed unreasonable.	Response: "What shall I do for you?"

4. Mary: "Do whatever he tells you."	Elijah: "Do as you have said."	
5. Jesus ordered jars filled with water and taken to the steward.		Elisha ordered jars brought and filled.
6. Order fulfilled.	Order fulfilled.	Order fulfilled.
7. Abundance of wine.	Abundance of meal and oil.	Abundance of oil.
8. Hospitality obligation paid.	Hospitality obligation paid.	Financial obligation paid.

The miracles of Elisha are similar enough to each other in instances where he provided for people, that the Johannine sign has parallels with all of them.[44] But the parallels involving women, both with Elijah and Elisha, are closer types from which the Johannine story was probably formed.

THE CENTURION'S SON

Jesus[45]   Elisha[46]

1. Official's son ill.   Army official had leprosy.

2. Came to Jesus for help.   Came to Elisha for help.

3. Jesus questioned his faith.

4. Jesus told him to leave;   Elisha sent messenger away to
his son was healed [distance   give directions [distance
healing].   healing].

                                   3. [John out of sequence]
                                   Officer doubted that this
                                   would work.

5. Officer believed and left.   Officer decided to follow
                                   directions.

6. Son (a child) was well.   Officer's flesh restored
                                   like that of a child.

Two other healing miracles Jesus performed took place at pools. The first man healed[47] expected to be dipped into the pool as Naaman was directed by Elisha to go and wash, but Jesus told him to get up, take his cot, and walk. The blind man at the Pool of Siloam,[48] however, was instructed to wash in the pool as Naaman had been told to bathe in the Jordan. Like

Naaman, after he had done so, he was healed; he had received his sight.

THE MULTIPLICATION OF THE LOAVES

Jesus[49]	Elisha[50]
1. Great crowd arrived at Passover time.	Sons of prophets gathered.
2. Andrew brought boy with barley loaves and fishes.[51]	Man from Baal-shalishah came with barley loaves and fresh grain.
3. Andrew, Jesus' disciple, said it was not enough.	Elisha's servant said there was not enough.
4. Jesus blessed the food and had it distributed.	Elisha commanded that the men be fed and promised that some would be left over.
5. All ate and were filled and twelve baskets full of food were left over.	All ate and they had some left over as Elijah promised.

There is some resemblance between these miracles and the occasion when Elijah multiplied the meal and oil for the widow.[52] In all instances, hospitality was required of people who apparently had not enough to provide it. In all cases the prophet involved performed a miracle which made the small amount of food there become more than enough.

NATURE MIRACLES

The power Jesus had over the forces of nature was evident in his ability to walk on the water.[53] The same power was shown by Elijah and Elisha when they divided the waters of the Jordan and walked across on dry land.[54] Elisha showed that he had a double portion of his master's spirit by also making an ax head float.[55] Details of these miracles are not very close.

RAISING THE DEAD

Jesus[56]	Elijah[57]	Elisha[58]
1. Jesus had special relationship with family at Bethany.	Elijah had received hospitality from the widow of Zerephath.	Elisha had received special hospitality from the Shunamite woman.

2. Lazarus became ill and died.	Widow's son became ill and died.	Shunamite woman's son became ill and died.
3. Mary and Martha blamed Jesus: "If you had been here, my brother would not have died."	Widow blamed Elijah for son's death.	Shunamite woman blamed Elisha for deceiving her by giving her a son and taking him away again.

Some details suggest that these similarities are more than coincidental. The picture of the Shunamite woman weeping at Elisha's feet after the death of her son[59] resembles Mary who fell at Jesus' feet after the death of her brother.[60] The resurrection miracle was the seventh miracle that Elisha performed and also the seventh that Jesus performed. Since Elisha had a double portion of Elijah's spirit, he also performed a second resurrection miracle, even after his death, when a corpse that touched his bones revived.[61] This was Elisha's fourteenth miracle. The miracles of Elisha follow a pattern that is similar to the miracles of Elijah. This does not mean that every miracle Elijah performed had exactly two counterparts in the Elisha stories. One has no parallel and another has four, but some are closer than others, and the total is exactly twice as many as Elijah had performed. The miracles of Jesus in the Fourth Gospel follow the typologies of Elijah and Elisha to about the same degree, being closer to the miracles of Elisha than Elijah.[62]

After Jesus fed the multitude with barley loaves as Elisha had done, the people referred to him as "the prophet."[63] In First and Second Kings, "the prophet" always refers to Elisha, never Elijah unaccompanied by his name.[64] Furthermore, Elisha was called the prophet in Samaria,[65] and Jesus, in Samaria, was recognized as a prophet.[66] The Pharisees asked John the Baptist if he were the Messiah, Elijah, or "the prophet."[67] "The prophet" following the new Elijah would have been the new Elisha, although, according to John as it now reads, the Baptist qualified for none of these. But after the ascension of Elijah, his disciples followed Elisha,[68] just as the disciples of John followed Jesus.[69] It was at the Jordan that John baptized so that Jesus might be revealed to "Israel." It was also there that John said he had seen the spirit descending upon Jesus.[70] It was also at the Jordan where Elijah gave up his mantle and Elisha received a double portion of Elijah's spirit.[71] After the ascension of Elijah fifty men "looked for him but they did not find him."[72] Jesus likewise told the Pharisees, "You will look for me, and you will not find me; where I am you cannot come."[73] Just as Elijah surrendered his leadership and disciples to Elisha, so John decreased while Jesus increased, and disciples of John became disciples of Jesus.[74]

The obvious question at this point is: If Jesus was interpreted as the new Elisha in the Gospel of John, why did he not perform fourteen miracles as Elisha had done. The answer is that originally the "signs" section in the Gospel of John may have existed as a separate document, including fourteen miracle stories attributed to Jesus. This then was later abridged; the number of miracles reduced to half; the prologue, the passion narrative, and the synoptic pericope[75] added to make a gospel out of a document patterned originally after First and Second Kings, or at least the section of those books containing the Elijah-Elisha narratives. This conjecture has by no means been proved, but this sort of hypothesis would help explain the unevenness in style and discontinuity of narrative now found in John. Many scholars have tried to reorganize the text to make the narrative continuous or explain its present lack of continuity.[76] It seems strange, for instance, for Jesus to have been in Jerusalem[77] and then to have crossed the Sea of Galilee[78] without traveling from Jerusalem to Galilee.

If the document had once been twice as large and composed of miracle stories, the editor who abridged the text probably had before him a text whose narrative was as unified geographically as the individual pericopes of John now are. But in choosing the seven best miracle stories, he necessarily broke the continuity. That the text as it is has been abridged and has omitted some of the signs is suggested by the summary in Jn 20:30 which Faure and Bultmann accept as part of the sign source: "Now Jesus did many other signs in the presence of the disciples which are not written in this book"--i.e. some were left out. Also the efforts to show that John the Baptist was not Elijah even though in many ways Jesus and John appear in the Gospel of John comparable to Elijah and Elisha, may indicate that the editor was intentionally omitting the Elijah sections of a book about John and Jesus as typologies of Elijah and Elisha. The original document may have shown both John and Jesus in the same critical relationship to Jerusalem leaders as

Elijah and Elisha had toward the national leaders at Samaria.

The close relationship between the Elijah-Elisha narratives and the signs in the Gospel of John shows a strong influence of HS literature as literary forms on the NT but it does not show that the Gospel of John was an imitation of the Hexateuch as the synoptic gospels. It now has a prologue to make it begin like a gospel and a passion narrative to make it end like a gospel, but it seems to have been pieced together from another kind of HS literature originally, just as the Gospel of Luke was made to fit into a life of Jesus from an original gospel. It shows, however, that the synoptic gospel writers were not the only NT authors to follow types--the author of the original Johannine narrative simply followed a type that was different from the one chosen by Matthew, Mark, and Luke. The way suggested that these gospels came to be, of course, is conjecture and not fact. The NT documents, as they now exist, are more or less like gospels and letters. Somehow some of them have been distorted to acquire their present form. Why? The answer to this question may be found in the influence of Marcion on the formation of the canon.

MARCION AND THE CANON

If Luke originally used a gospel as a source for his life of Jesus, where did he get the gospel? One possibility is that he used the same gospel of Luke that Marcion canonized. This is no new suggestion. Knox has convincingly argued that it makes more sense to assume that the church later modified Marcion's teachings by adding to his gospel a number of contrary Jewish teachings than to assume that Marcion had the Gospel of Luke as we now have it, but that he reduced it by about fifty percent so as to remove all the Jewish elements.[79]

The fact that the document as it now is includes many Jewish teachings that were not in Marcion's Gospel of Luke does not automatically require the change to have been made one way or the other, but it indicates that editorial work was done. It is also true that some of these Jewish elements, like the Semitic prologue in Luke, destroy the hexateuchal pattern and at the same time present a pseudo-epistle which includes a "life of Jesus." According to the Gospel pattern deduced in this study, the gospel before the present "life of Jesus" replaced the Sermon on the Mount with Jesus' sermon in his own home town. Marcion did not want a repetition of the law given by Moses. Like Paul, he was interested in a gospel of liberation--not an emphasis on law. Much of the content of the Sermon on the Mount is well organized into Luke's "Deuteronomy" section--but it was not done haphazardly as scholars have sometimes held. Even if it could be proved that the document attributed to Luke was not dependent upon Marcion's gospel, it would be necessary to presume that there was some gospel written before Luke upon which the present document was dependent.

Knox's proposal was that Marcion was such a powerful leader in the church that the division of the church in Rome that excommunicated him could not ignore him. Since he had established the first canon of the NT, they had either to anathamatize his whole canon or else neutralize it by additions. They chose the latter, forming a canon that included only gospels and epistles, together with the unifying document, "The Acts of the Apostles."[80] Since Marcion's canon included only the Gospel of Luke and ten letters of Paul, the church added to the canon other letters and gospels,[81] but it is clear that the church strained to fit the literature they wanted in the canon into these two categories.

The Book of Revelation, for instance, begins with letters to the seven churches, but it is really not a letter. It is an apocalyptic prophecy that is distinctly pro-Jewish which also means anti-Marcion. The Epistles of James and Hebrews are really not letters either. They are more like the wisdom literature of the HS than epistles. They are also pro-Jewish in logic and doctrine. It might be worth an imaginary reconstruction to consider the type of literature the church possessed before Marcion. The most normal kind of literature for a new religion to compose would be patterned after the literature of the group from which it originated. Thus the ritual of the United Methodist Discipline is very similar to the ritual of the Episcopal Book of Common Prayer, which also resembles the Roman Catholic Missal. The HS was the literature familiar to the authors of the NT; it provided a basis for early Christian faith and practice. Without some historical event of dramatic proportions, one would expect the new Jewish movement to have produced literature similar to the type it imitated. The Bar Cochba rebellion followed by Marcion's rejection of Jewish influences seems to account for this deviation.

JOHN AND THE SYNOPTIC GOSPELS

Scholars have never been satisfied with solutions they have conjectured that related John to the
synoptic gospels. There are clearly some themes and
even exact wording, sometimes, to suggest a relationship, but the Fourth Gospel is a different kind of
literature from the synoptic gospels. Morton Smith has
shown that there is a close relationship of events in
sequence between parts of the "Secret Gospel of Mark"
which he discovered and parts of the Fourth Gospel.
This is specially true of the Markan parallel to the
story of the raising of Lazarus and the feeding of the
multitude.[83] Smith concluded, "Yet both the parallel
episodes and the parallel geographical notices differ
so widely from each other in wording and in many details that it is almost impossible to think either
Gospel based on the other."[84]

If, however, the Johannine stories of the miracles associated with John and Jesus had been written
independently of the Secret Gospel of Mark, a later
editor, trying to change this collection of stories to
make them appear as part of a gospel, might have organized the material he planned to retain from these
stories into the same basic outline where other ver-
sions of the same stories appeared in other gospels.
This would be true of the feeding of the multitude and
the Lazarus stories. Since the editor would have added
both the prologue and the passion narrative, it is not
surprising that there are some close parallels between
these two parts and similar parts of other gospels.
Neirynck has made a convincing case for believing that
the empty tomb stories of Matthew and John are sufficiently similar to lead to the belief that the author
of John used Matthew as his source.[85] Walker argued
strongly for the dependence of the Johannine prayer in
John 17 on the Lord's prayer in Matthew 6.[86] There is
still one other close resemblance between the Gospels
of Matthew and John.

The setting for the multiplication of the
loaves and the dissertation on the bread from heaven
in John 6 seems to have been patterned after the setting for the Sermon on the Mount in Matthew 5, as the
following quotations will show:

Matthew	John
	After these things Jesus went away across the Sea

	of Galilee of Tiberias. A great crowd
Now when Jesus saw the crowds,	followed him, because they saw the signs which he was doing on the sick people. Now, Jesus
he went up into the mountain,	went away into the mountain, and sat
and after he had sat down, his disciples came to him (Matt 5:1).	down with his disciples (6:1-3).

Between the end of John 5 and the beginning of John 6, there is an obvious "seam." In John 5, Jesus was in Jerusalem. In John 6, he was on a mountain near the Sea of Galilee, but there is no narrative reporting how Jesus got from Jerusalem to Galilee. It looks as if some editor was trying to make a gospel out of a historical prophecy. Since he had to reduce the number of stories he included[87] he omitted the miracles that then followed John 5, took John 6 from whatever position it had previously held and put it in the same place in his outline that the feeding of the five thousand held in the Markan outline, but he wanted to give it a central significance, so he structured a setting for his bread of heaven miracle on a mountain, similar to Matthew's Sermon on the Mount. This suggests that it was not the author of the original collection of miracle stories who created those verbal parallels and parallels of outline that have been found here and there in the Fourth Gospel. These are all outside the limits of the "sign source." They appear in places where there are other signs of editorializing.

The miracle stories related about the new Elijah and Elisha would have been composed before the time of Marcion, when it would have seemed in order to compose any literature following the typologies of HS literature--law, history, prophecy, wisdom literature, psalms, and apocalypses. After the Bar Cochba revolt of A. D. 132-135, however, Marcion led a strong anti-Jewish movement. As part of his program, he prepared the first Christian canon which included the Gospel of Luke and the ten letters of Paul. This seems like a strange canon for a new religious group, and it probably would have been different had it not been for the Bar Cochba Revolt. As it was, however, Marcion was a sufficiently strong leader that those who wanted to reduce his influence could not ignore him. Since Marcion had won Roman confidence, the rest of the Christian church found it expedient to give the appearance of having accepted his canon and basic points of view, but at the same time, it introduced many strong Jewish works and points of view.

The church had to begin with his canon and rejudaize Christianity by adding other letters and gospels. They did this by adding such pro-Jewish materials as the Johannine epistles, First and Second Peter, James, Jude, Hebrews, and the Book of Revelation. They also added the Gospels of Matthew and Mark, but not all of these materials were gospels and epistles, originally. Hebrews was a homiletic midrash; James was a type of wisdom literature, like Proverbs or Ecclesiastes; Revelation 4:1-22:5 was an apocalyptic prophecy, like Daniel; the Book of Acts seems to have been an antitype of the Book of Judges and First Samuel; but all of these were forced into letters or gospels in one way or another. Marcion's Gospel of Luke was destroyed as a gospel and made into a life of Jesus, although even this document began as a letter to Theophilus. In order to admit some Johannine literature into the canon, this conjectured narrative of the new Elijah and Elisha had either to be made into a gospel or a letter. The editor involved chose the former, but he left some traces of his editorial policy.

The editing of all of these documents was probably done after Marcion's canon had become popular. That was a period when Christians had to establish their identity in relationship both to Judaism and to Rome. Without the temple, both Christianity and rabbinic Judaism had to concentrate on literature, as Jews had done in the Babylonian captivity years before. The first reaction to the bloody Bar Cochba Revolt that had been based on a holy war theology was that of Marcion's: Christians do not believe in holy war, and they are in no way related to this neurotic holy war theology. The second reaction was more balanced and representative, trying to include literature from all sects of Christianity, but forcing these documents into the canon outline established by Marcion.

The new Hexateuch, which still seems evident in Matthew and is reflected in Mark and Luke, was evidently known long before Marcion. By then it was a form later editors had to imitate, but they knew something about this literary form, just as they also knew about other literature that had been composed according to the pattern of HS books that they respected.

115

THE ACTS OF THE APOSTLES

There is one more argument to support the thesis that a gospel originally was a document patterned after the Hexateuch. This is the content of The Acts of the Apostles. The books in the HS that follow the Hexateuch are books of history, like Judges, First and Second Samuel, and First and Second Kings. Joshua ends with the children of Israel established in the land after Joshua had died. Leaders that followed were charismatic. They had not been born into dynasties that were already established. Instead, there were temporary leaders, like Gideon, Jephthah, and Samson-- all of whom had been stirred by the spirit of the Lord to lead the community. The most important of these leaders was Saul whose experiences with the spirit called him into leadership of all Israel, and he held that position until his death, after which David became king.

The Acts of the Apostles is also a book of history that begins after the death of the new Joshua with a group of charismatic leaders who had been aroused by the Holy Spirit to lead the developing church. The most important of these was Paul, whom Acts alone claimed was formerly called Saul. Like the earlier Saul, the new Saul was overcome by the Holy Spirit to become a leader--almost against his will. As Saul set about unifying the tribes of Israel, so the new Saul went out to the diaspora to bring together the Jews in the diaspora in preparation for the establishment of the kingdom.

The Book of Acts breaks off before the new Saul had died and the new David had come to power. No one is quite certain why this was done, but one reason might have been that the son of David had not come into his kingdom during the lifetime of the author. Therefore he could not follow the typology any further than up to the point near the end of the death of the new Saul. This included an antitype of Judges and the first part of First Samuel. Acts, however, had been composed on the basis that the history up to the period immediately following the death of the new Joshua had already been written. This means there was already a new Hexateuch, which the committee on canon placed in order just before the Acts of the Apostles, just as the Hexateuch had been organized before Judges and other books of early Israelite history.

There is no question that typology was a strong force in the formation of early Christian belief, prophecy, and formation of literature. Early Christians believed that there would be a renewal of the kingdom in their day just as there had been after the captivities of Egypt and Babylon. They strained facts to prove that all of the signs of their day fit earlier patterns. Part of that effort seems to be reflected in their creation of a literary form they called a gospel. Although they were not able to shape all of their literary data into a rigid form that exactly fit every item of earlier history in the exact sequence, in the Gospel of Matthew there are enough parallels in sequence to think that this was not purely accidental. These paralleled events from early Hebrew beginnings in Genesis to those related to Joshua up to the time he renewed the contract and died. Partly in an effort to make other literature conform closely to Matthew, Mark was expanded to include more Matthaean teachings, and John was seriously revised to begin and end about the way Matthew did and be about the same length. How we wish we could have seen all of these documents before they had been reedited! Unfortunately, that is not possible, so we will have to depend on some rather fanciful conjectures such as the ones offered here.

By the time of Irenaeus, the term, "gospel," was used to describe one or all of the four gospels. As a group, the collection was called "the fourfold gospel" (tetramorphon to euaggelion)[88] or just "the gospel" (to euaggelion).[89] Clement of Alexandria[90] mentioned a Zechariah, father of John, reported "in the gospels" (en tois euaggeliois) even though it is found only in Luke. In order to distinguish one gospel from the rest, the name to which the document had been attributed was added, for example, secundum Matthaeum, Marcum, Lucam, or Joannem.[91] Irenaeus said that Luke, Paul's follower, put down a book, the gospel which had been preached by Paul.[92] It is evident, therefore, that the term, "gospel," was used to describe the message which early Christians proclaimed; but it is also true that four of the books in the Christian canon were called "gospels." The term, gospel, meant "good news," and when used in a Christian context, it referred to the "good news of the kingdom" announced by Jesus, the Messiah. But how did this term, gospel, come to characterize a type of literature, and what type of literature did it characterize? What distinguished a "gospel" from an essay, for instance, or a biography, a letter, a prophecy, a psalm, or a religious history? Does a gospel have a literary form that

117

distinguishes it from all other types of literature?[93] For this question there has previously been no satisfactory answer.

Many scholars have considered a gospel to be a biography, but they usually explain that it is not the kind of biography twentieth century readers are accustomed to call biography. Some have called it an aretalogy, and others have simply denied that it was anything definable. This study has undertaken an approach that is different from any of the earlier attempts.[94] Instead of trying to begin with the _form_, we began by examining _ideas_ and _thought-forms_ of the people who wrote gospels and then considered how they developed into a form. At first there seems no reasonable relationship between the literary form, "gospel," and the Jewish concept of time, culture, and thought-form. A closer examination, however, shows that the beliefs, typology, and nationalistic zeal that prompted Second Isaiah to write poetry, announcing the gospel of a new exodus and the restoration of the promised land, prompted other writers with similar hopes and views to announce the good news again through a literary medium patterned after earlier literature that told the history of the good news.

CONCLUSIONS

Daube was correct when he said that the exodus pattern was the most important pattern of deliverance in the Bible. This became a basic type that continued to carry with it the belief that God would apply the same rules of release for his nation as was required of Jews who set their debtor slaves free on Jubilee years. Carmichael was also probably correct in reasoning that Deuteronomy formed its laws on the release of Hebrew debtor slaves on the basis of the report of the liberation of Exodus. Israelites believed strongly that God's acts in previous history provided the basis for determining present ethics. The ancient belief that time moved in cycles established a philosophical background against which exodus typology could become still more sophisticated and provide a basis for predicting the future. This was done as early as the Babylonian captivity.

The firm belief that time moves in cycles was influential in developing in Judaism the eschatological doctrine of good news. Since Jews could trace their national recurrence through three cycles, they were convinced that the old Gentile age would pass away and the new Jewish age would circle around in its place, restoring the United Kingdom to its pristine glory with a messianic king ruling from Jerusalem.

Early Jewish and Christian dogmatic theologians were not objective research scholars trying to see the most likely interpretation of all the data. They began with a conviction and searched everywhere in the scripture for material to prove that their conviction was correct. This meant picking carefully that which supported their case and leaving untouched all data that pointed in another direction. They forced conclusions that did not really fit, such as making four hundred, twenty-two years fulfill the requirements of four hundred, ninety years. If they really had held that cycles repeated themselves exactly, they would have waited patiently until another four hundred years had passed in "Egypt," forty years in "the wilderness," and a long period for "the conquest," after the land had been taken from them, but that is not what they did. Before ten years had passed after Jews lost possession of the land to the Romans, they began to count Sabbaths and Jubilees and match current events with the last three and a half years of the evil, Gentile age.

If Jews had not had a dogma of the good news there may have been a biography of Jesus, but there would never have developed a literary form called a gospel. The author of Hebrews told his readers, "We have received the gospel as also they."[95] The people referred to as "they" were the Hebrews who left Egypt and came to the borders of the promised land. These people erred by tempting the Lord. They sent spies to see if the invasion they had been commanded to undertake was reasonable. Since the author of Hebrews thought he and his contemporaries were in exactly the same spot in the cycle of destiny, he strongly urged his readers not to sin as their ancestors had done, lest they also be condemned to die in the wilderness.

The gospel which the author of Hebrews received was the typological equivalent of the gospel the early Hebrews received when they left Egypt and the gospel Second Isaiah announced from Babylon. This announcement and belief motivated the author of Hebrews to bring together all of the scriptural proof he could muster to convince his readers of the way they should behave. He did this by composing a sermon on Psalm 110. The authors of the synoptic gospels were just as strongly convinced as was the author of Hebrews, but they structured their documents differently.

When Second Isaiah announced to Zion that Cyrus of Persia was about to conquer Babylon and the Davidic kingdom would soon be established, this was called announcing "good news." Prophets of NT times calculated and matched typologies of their age with those of the Egyptian and the Babylonian cycles until they had an extensive collection of events related to the activities of Jesus that could be matched in sequence with books of the Hexateuch as Matthew had done. It is not surprising that Christians called this document "good news."

Although it was similar to some secular documents that were called "bios," or "life" of some hero, the literary form given to each of these documents was not primarily a biography or an aretalogy. If they qualify as "lives" of Jesus, they are special kinds of lives. They were not only lives; that is probably the reason they were not called lives of Jesus. The pattern to which these documents were made to conform had its own special outline, and it was called a gospel. Given Jewish convictions at that time, this was "proof" that the Kingdom of Heaven was at hand. Some of their reasons for accepting this document as proof were these:

1) Jews believed that there was nothing in the world that was not in the scripture. Therefore those who tried to predict the future had the Hebrew Scripture as their only source of data. 2) They believed there was no before and after in scripture. Therefore they were free to take events out of historical sequence and match them with the recognized archetype from the Hexateuch. 3) They believed that all prophecy would be fulfilled in the days of the Messiah, and these were days of the Messiah. 4) Matthew had shown over and over again how these events that he narrated fulfilled that which had been prophesied earlier. 5) They believed that two or three witnesses were enough to prove a case. 6) Matthew had supported many of his claims with two proof texts, two parables, or two chreias. 7) Jews believed that time moved in circles in a certain prescribed sequence. Through the Gentile age, it moved from captivity to wilderness to conquest to rule. This is what happened between the Egyptian exodus and the Solomonic kingdom. This happened between the destruction of the temple in 586 B.C. and either the reestablishment of the temple under Ezra and Nehemiah or the rededication of the temple under the rule of the Hasmoneans in 164 B.C. 8) Matthew had traced history through the Hexateuch until the renewal

of the contract, matching hexateuchal archetypes with current types related to the life and ministry of Jesus. The document he produced on the basis of these convictions was called "the gospel."

The methodology Matthew followed was approved, and his conclusions were convincing to those who accepted these doctrines. Other documents patterned like it were also called gospels. These were literary documents that were designed to prove that the kingdom was about to be restored. Since the events that provided the antitypes were associated with the activities and teachings of Jesus, the Messiah, these were called the gospels of the Lord, Jesus the Messiah. They were not called biographies, lives of Jesus, aretalogies, or encomiums, although there are many characteristics of the gospels that are also found in these other kinds of literature. They were not called biographies, apparently, because the primary emphasis was not on the details of Jesus's life but the good news of the kingdom. Because it was necessary to use the Hexateuch as an archetype to reach approved detailed conclusions, the gospel as a literary form was recognized as a new Hexateuch and later editors of the "gospel" of John had to reorganize that document to make it look like a Hexateuch to become approved as a gospel. The Acts of the Apostles was evidently patterned after Judges and First Samuel so that it could follow literary gospels in the canon, just as Judges and First Samuel followed the Hexateuch.

It is true that the gospel writers lived in the Greco-Roman world and were aware of Greek literary forms. As Shuler has shown, there are aspects of the Gospel of Matthew that resemble an encomium biography, and there are seventeen miracles in the Gospel of Mark that can be fairly called <u>aretai</u>, but Shuler was right, when, after he had presented all his arguments for holding that Matthew was a biography, concluded, "What Matthew desires from his audience is indeed praise of Jesus; but, even more important to him is this faith response. The <u>topoi</u> and the techniques he has used are designed to elicit this response and to instruct the believer in the course he or she is to follow."[96] This study has been an attempt to examine that which was "even more important" than "praise of Jesus." That which was more important was the gospel of the Kingdom of Heaven. According to Matthew's logic, the signs reflected in previous cycles of time indicated that Jesus was the Messiah around whom this kingdom would be formed. Because the gospel was more important than praise of the Messiah, each of these early documents that was patterned after the Hexateuch was called a "gospel" rather than a _vita_ or a _bios_ of Jesus.

No effort has been made here to show how much or how little the works of others have succeeded in showing that the gospels were biographies or something else.[97] This study has attempted to learn how the term "gospel" came to be applied to these literary documents and what the distinguishing characteristics of a gospel are. The data examined seem to point in the direction of the conclusions given, but these are necessarily conjectural and speculative.

In this study some things are more conjectural than others. The concepts of cyclical time and typological interpretation in NT times are not conjectural at all. They existed as historical facts and were practiced. The conjecture that the gospels were written around the concept of a Hexateuch is probable. The supposition that the typological parallels among the Hexateuch, Second Isaiah, and the gospels were originally intended in about the form suggested here is possible, but these can hardly be tested for accuracy. Our success in guessing depends upon our suppositions of the kinds of parallels Jews and Christians considered valid two thousand years ago. It is almost certain that some of these identifications are wrong, but it is difficult to say which ones. Still more tenuous are the general theories constructed to explain how the documents came to be the way they are when they fail to fit the hexateuchal type perfectly. Nevertheless, both the facts and the possibilities are thought-provoking, and perhaps even edifying. Readers will probably differ on the degree to which they concur with the judgments made. I am always grateful to readers who will devote the time required to examine my arguments, even if they disagree with my theories and conclusions.

ENDNOTES

1.   John 1:9-10.
2.   Gen 1:1-26.
3.   John 1:4.
4.   John 1:5
5.   John 1:9
6.   Exod 3:2-6.
7.   John 1:14, 18; Exod 16:7, 10; 24:16; 34:6.
8.   John 1:14.
9.   Exod 34:6 LXX renders freely <u>polyeleos</u> <u>kai</u> <u>alethenos</u>, which is reflected also in John 1:14: <u>pleres</u> <u>charitos</u> <u>kai</u> <u>aletheias</u>.
10. John 12:1 ff.
11. 1 Kgs 17:1-6.
12. 2 Kgs 2:14.
13. 1 Kgs 17:8-16.
14. 2 Kgs 2:19-23.
15. 1 Kgs 17:17-24.
16. 2 Kgs 2:23-24.
17. 1 Kgs 18:1-40.
18. 2 Kgs 3:13-20.
19. 2 Kgs 1:9-10.
20. 2 Kgs 4:1-7.
21. 2 Kgs 1:11-12.
22. 2 Kgs 4:8-17.
23. 2 Kgs 2:8.
24. 2 Kgs 4:18-37.
25. 2 Kgs 4:38-41.
26. 2 Kgs 4:42-44.
27. 2 Kgs 5:1-14.
28. 2 Kgs 5:19-27.
29. 2 Kgs 6:1-7.
30. 2 Kgs 6:15-19.
31. 2 Kgs 13:21.
32. 2 Kgs 2:9-12.
33. So also Sirach 48:12.
34. John 2:1-11.
35. John 4:46-54.
36. John 5:2-9.
37. John 6:4-14.
38. John 6:16-21.
39. John 9:1-7.
40. John 11:1-44.
41. John 2:1-11.
42. 1 Kgs 17:1-6.
43. 2 Kgs 4:1-7.
44. 2 Kgs 2:19-20; 3:13-20; 4:38-41.
45. John 4:46-54.
46. 2 Kgs 5:1-14.

47. John 5:2-9.
48. John 9:1-7.
49. John 6:4-14.
50. 2 Kgs 4:42-44.
51. John is the only gospel that agrees with 2 Kgs in specifying that barley loaves were multiplied.
52. 1 Kgs 17:1-6.
53. John 6:16-21.
54. 2 Kgs 2:8, 14.
55. John 6:1-7.
56. John 11:1-44.
57. 1 Kgs 17:17-24.
58. 2 Kgs 4:18-37.
59. 2 Kgs 4:27.
60. John 11:32.
61. 2 Kgs 13:21. Jesus's resurrection after death may have been understood as a great improvement over Elisha's resurrection of a corpse that touched his own. If so, this was included as an additional miracle above the seven otherwise listed.
62. Several efforts have been made to compare the Gospel of John with the Exodus typology, comparing the signs of John with the plagues of Egypt, and considering Jesus as a prophet to be a second Moses. H. Sellin, Zur Typologie des Johannesevangeliums (Uppsala, 1950); J. J. Enz, "The Book of Exodus as a Literary Type for the Gospel of John," JBL 76 (1957):208-15; R. H. Smith, "Exodus Typology in the Fourth Gospel," JBL 81 (1962):329-42.

Some of these suggestions are thought-provoking and may be correct. It is possible for an author to have had John and Jesus parallel Aaron and Moses at the same time they paralleled Elijah and Elisha and even Eli and Samuel, for that matter. But the parallels such as the book of the contract (Exod 20-30) and the "New Commandment" of John 18:34 and Moses's finishing his work (Exod 40:33b) with "It is finished" of John 19:30 (Enz, pp. 210-211) or comparing the water turned to blood with the water turned to wine (Exod 7:14-24; John 2:1-11) (Smith, p. 338) are not such striking parallels as the miracles of Elijah and Elisha. The healing of the official's son (John 4:46-54), for instance, is a closer parallel to the healing of the officer by proxy at a distance by Elisha (2 Kgs 5:1-4) than to the plague on animals (Exod 9:17) as Smith suggests (p. 338). C. Goodwin, "How Did John Treat his Sources," JBL 73 (1954):62, noted, "Five times he refers to the Prophet that was to come, but he never quotes Dt 18:15 ff."
63. John 6:14.
64. Such as 1 Kgs 18:36. For Elisha see 2 Kgs 20:22; 5:13; 6:12; 9:4.
65. 2 Kgs 5:3.
66. John 4:19.
67. John 1:25.
68. 2 Kgs 2:15-18.

69. John 1:37.
70. John 1:29-34.
71. 2 Kgs 2:6-15.
72. 2 Kgs 2:17.
73. John 7:34.
74. John 3:30
75. John 7:53-8:11.
76. R. Bultmann, Das Evangelium des Johannes (Goettingen, 1957), passim; C. K. Barrett, The Gospel according to John (London: 1955), pp. 18-21; Wilkens, Die Entstehungs geschichte des vierten Evangeliums (Zollinkno, c1958), pp. 4-5, 30; O. Merlier, Le Quatrieme Evangile (Paris, 1961), pp. 426-47, 429-30; Faure, "Die Alttestamentlichen Zitate im 4 Evangelium und die Quellenschneidungshypothese," ZNW 21 (1922):99-122; P. Parker, "Two Editions of John," JBL 75 (1956):303-14; B. Noack, Zur Johanneseischen Tradition (Kopenhagen, 1954), passim; and S. Temple, "A Key to the Composition of the Fourth Gospel," JBL (1961):221-32.
77. John 5:1.
78. John 6:1.
79. J. Knox, Marcion and the New Testament (Chicago, 1942). See especially pages 77-113.
80. Knox, Ibid., pp. 126-39.
81. Ibid., 157.
83. M. Smith, The Secret Gospel (New York, c1973), pp. 45-62.
84. Ibid., p.60.
85. F. Neirynck, "John and the Synoptics: The Empty Tomb Stories," an unpublished paper read at the SNTS meeting at Leuven, Belgium, Aug. 25, 1982.
86. W. O. Walker, Jr., "The Lord's Prayer in Matthew and John," NTS 28 (1982):237-56. P. Parker, "Luke and the Fourth Evangelist," NTS 9 (1963):317-36, compared data in Luke and John not found in other gospels. Also John and Matthew and John and Mark. He concluded that Luke and John were acquainted with much material, unknown to other gospel writers. M. E. Boismard, "Saint Luc et la Redaction du Quatrieme Evangile," RB 69 (1962):185-211, has argued convincingly that Luke was an editor who revised Marcion's gospel and wrote salutations at the beginning of both Luke and Acts. This much general editing must have been done as the canon was being determined—sometime after Marcion, and "Luke" may have been chairman of the committee on canon. This, of course, is pretty extensive and imaginary conjecturing with a small amount of data.
87. John 20:30.
88. Irenaeus, 3.xi.8 (MPG 7.885b, 889).
89. Eusebius, HE 5.24.6
90. Strom. 1.21.145.B.
91. Irenaeus 1.xi.7 (MPG 7.884).
92. Irenaeus 1.i (MPG 7.845a).

93. G. Friedrich, "Euaggelion" Theologisches Woerterbuch zum Neuen Testament (Stuttgart, 1935) II, pp. 718-734, ignored the question of a gospel as a literary form.

94. One of the most recent scholars to examine the subject is P. L. Shuler, A Genre for the Gospels (Philadelphia, c1982). Shuler studied the major attempts that had been made before, concluded that none of them was adequate, and proved to his own satisfaction that a gospel resembled the form Greek rhetoricians called an encomium. This was a eulogy attributed to great characters, and Shuler considered it a kind of biography. Therefore he concluded that it is fair to call gospels biographies. Albert Schweitzer, The Quest of the Historical Jesus, tr. W. Montgomery (New York, c1968), p. 3, said, "We, on our part, have reason to be grateful to the early Christians that, in the consequence of this attitude they handed down to us, not biographies of Jesus but only Gospels, and that therefore we possess the Idea and Person with the minimum of historical and contemporary limitations."

95. Heb 4:2

96. Shuler, Genre, p. 106.

97. Those interested in a survey of the arguments and theories of others who have tried to define a gospel might check Shuler, Genre.

BIBLIOGRAPHY

B. C. Bacon, Studies in Matthew (New York, c1950).

D. L. Baker, "Typology and the Christian Use of the Old Testament," SJT 29 (1976):149.

C. K. Barrett, The Gospel according to John (London: 1955), pp. 18-21.

Baumgaertel, "The Hermeneutical Problem of the Old Testament," Essays, pp. 134-59; Eichrodt, "Typological," Essays, 240-42.

M. Bergman, "Another Reference to 'A Teacher of Righteousness' in Midrashic Literature," RQ 37 (1979):97-98.

M. E. Boismard, "Saint Luc et la Redaction du Quatrieme Evangile," RB 69 (1962):185-211.

GWB, The Consequences of the Covenant (Leiden, 1970), pp. 9-18.

GWB, Jesus: the King and his Kingdom (Macon, 1984), pp. 253-83.

GWB, "The Priestly Teacher of Righteousness," RQ 6 (1969):553-58; "The Office of the Teacher of Righteousness," RQ 9 (1977):415-25.

GWB, Revelation and Redemption (Dillsboro: sold by Mercer U. Press, 1978).

GWB, To the Hebrews (Garden City, 1972), pp. 52-83.

R. Bultmann, Das Evangelium des Johannes (Goettingen, 1957).

R. Bultmann, "Ursprung und Sinn der Typologie as hermeneutische Methode," TLZ 75 (1950):205-12.

B. C. Butler, The Originality of St. Matthew (Cambridge, 1951).

C. Carmichael, Law and Narrative in the Bible (Ithaca, 1985), pp. 82-83.

C. Carmichael, "A New View of the Origin of the Deuteronomic Credo," VT 16 (1969):273-89.

J. Danielou, From Shadow to Reality, tr. W. Hibberd (London, c1960); W. Eichrodt, Theology of the Old Testament, 2 vols., tr. J. A. Baker (Philadelphia, 1967);

D. Daube, "The Earliest Structure of the Gospels," NTS 5 (1958/59):174-87.

D. Daube, The Exodus Pattern in the Bible (London, 1963).

R. M. Davidson, Typology in Scripture (Berrien Springs, Mich., c1981).

Mk 11:18. C. H. Dodd, New Testament Studies (Manchester, c1954).

J. Drury, Tradition and Design in Luke's Gospel (London, c1976).

W. Eichrodt, "Is Typological Exegesis an Appropriate Method?", tr. J. Barr, Essays, p. 225.

J. J. Enz, "The Book of Exodus as a Literary Type for the Gospel of John," JBL 76 (1957):208-15.

C. F. Evans, "The Central Section of Luke's Gospel," Studies in the Gospels (Oxford, 1957).

P. Fairbairn, The Typology of Scripture (Grand Rapids, n. d.).

A. Farrer, "On Dispensing with Q," Studies in the Gospels, ed. D. E. Nineham (Oxford, 1955), pp. 75-77.

A. Farrer, St. Matthew and St. Mark (Philadelphia, 1954).

Faure, "Die Alttestamentlichen Zitate im 4 Evangelium und die Quellenschneidungshypothese," ZNW 21 (1922):99-122.

G. Friedrich, "Euaggelion" Theologisches Woerterbuch zum Neuen Testament (Stuttgart, 1935) II, pp. 718-734.

M. Gaster, The Samaritans (London, 1925).

E. Goodenough, By Light, Light (New Haven, 1935).

C. Goodwin, "How Did John Treat his Sources," JBL 73 (1954):62.

L. Goppelt, Typos: the Typological Interpretation of the Old Testament in the New, tr. D. H. Madvig, foreword, E. E. Ellis (Grand Rapids, 1982).

M. D. Goulder, Type and History (London, 1964).

A. Harnack, Marcion, Das Evangelium vom fremden Gott (Leipzig, 1924), pp. 215-33.

128

W. A. Irwin, "A Still Small Voice . . . Said, What are You Doing Here?" JBL 78 (1959):9.

J. D. Kingsbury, Matthew: Structure, Christology, Kingdom (Philadelphia, c1975), p. 3, fn. 13.

J. Knox, Marcion and the New Testament (Chicago, 1942).

G. W. H. Lampe and K. J. Woollcombe, Essays on Typology (London: SCM Press, c1957), pp. 60-61).

T. R. W. Longstaff, "Crisis and Christology: the Theology of Mark," W. R. Farmer (ed.), New Synoptic Studies (Macon, c1983):373-92.

J. Macdonald, The Samaritan Theology (Philadelphia, c1964).

J. Manek, "The New Exodus in the Books of Luke," Nov 2 (1958):8-23.

O. Merlier, Le Quatrieme Evangile (Paris, 1961), pp. 426-47, 429-30.

F. Neirynck, "John and the Synoptics: The Empty Tomb Stories," an unpublished paper read at the SNTS meeting at Leuven, Belgium, Aug. 25, 1982.

D. E. Nineham, "The Order of Events in St. Mark's Gospel—an Examination of Dr. Dodd's Hypothesis," Studies in the Gospels (Oxford, 1957).

B. Noack, Zur Johanneseischen Tradition (Kopenhagen, 1954), passim.

P. Parker, "Luke and the Fourth Evangelist," NTS 9 (1963):317-36.

P. Parker, "Two Editions of John," JBL 75 (1956):303-14.

G. Von Rad, "Typological Interpretation of the Old Testament," tr. J. Bright, C. Westermann (ed.), Essays on Old Testament Hermeneutics (Richmond, c1963), p. 22.

Ibid. pp. 22-23; C. Westerman, "The Interpretation of the Old Testament," Essays, pp. 40-43.

B. Reicke, "Instruction and Discussion in the Travel Narrative," Studia Evangelica 1 (1959):206-16). .

James Sanders, Torah and Canon (Philadelphia, c1972).

O. J. F. Seitz, "What Do These Stones Mean?" JBL 79 (1960):247–54.

A. Schweitzer, The Quest of the Historical Jesus, tr. W. Montgomery (New York, c1968).

H. Sellin, Zur Typologie des Johannesevangeliums (Upsala, 1950).

J. S. Semler, Versuch einer freiern theologischen Lehrart (Halle: C. H. Hemmerle, 1777), p. 86, fn. 96.

P. L. Shuler, A Genre for the Gospels (Philadelphia, c1982).

M. Smith, The Secret Gospel (New York, c1973), pp. 45–62.

R. H. Smith, "Exodus Typology in the Fourth Gospel," JBL 81 (1962):329–42.

D. F. Strauss, The Life of Jesus (London and New York, 1895).

S. Temple, "A Key to the Composition of the Fourth Gospel," JBL (1961):221–32.

R. C. Trench, Notes on the Parables of our Lord (London, 1870), pp. 12–147. Von Rad, Essays, p. 23.

W. Vischer, The Witness of the Old Testament to Christ, tr. A. B. Crabtree (London, 1949); and G. Von Rad, Old Testament Theology, 2 vols, tr. D. M. G. Stalker (New York, 1962).

W. O. Walker, Jr., "The Lord's Prayer in Matthew and John," NTS 28 (1982):237–56.

Wilkens, Die Entstehungs geschichte des vierten Evangeliums (Zollinkno, c1958).

H. W. Wolff, "The Hermeneutics of the Old Testament," Essays, p. 174.

INDEX

Words in this index are inclusive. Singulars include plurals, and all derivitives; present tense verbs include all other tenses and forms.

132

136

```
Troop                                                          68
Trumpet                                                     8, 10
Type                  vii, 3, 4, 5, 6, 12, 13, 14 19, 20,
                             24, 82, 111, 118, 121
Typological    2, 7, 11, 18, 22, 25, 27, 29, 31, 34, 42, 43, 122
Typology      v, vii, x, 3, 4, 5, 12, 13, 15, 16, 21, 24, 26,
                 27, 31, 38, 41, 42, 101, 109, 110, 116, 117,
                                   118, 119, 120, 124
Typtein                                                         3
Tyre                                                        1, 11

Unclean            48, 65, 66, 68, 69, 70, 88, 89, 90, 92
Ur                                                            101

Vindication                                                93, 99
Vineyard                                               55, 92, 94
Vischer                        vii, 15, 16, 17, 37, 42, 60
Von Rad                       vii, 15, 18, 19, 37, 38, 102

Walker                                                   113, 125
Warn                                                           55
Weeden                                                         85
Westermann                                           vii, 15, 37
Western                                                    x, 251
Wilderness     11, 12, 13, 16, 18, 19, 23, 24, 29, 31, 34, 46,
                     47, 52, 55, 64, 65, 71, 87, 88, 94, 97,
                                   99, 104, 119, 120
Wilkens                                                       125
Wisdom                                                        112
Witness                                                       120
Wife                                                           54
Woe                                                            89
Wolff                                                      18, 38
Woolcombe                                               4, 6, 35

Zadok                                                           9
Zeal                                                 7, 33, 118
Zechariah                                                      93
Zerephath                                                     108
Zerubbabel                                                  1, 31
Zimri                                                           7
Zion                                                          120
```